ILLUMINATING THE PATH
TO ENLIGHTENMENT

ILLUMINATING THE PATH TO ENLIGHTENMENT

Tenzin Gyatso
HIS HOLINESS
THE FOURTEENTH DALAI LAMA OF TIBET

A COMMENTARY ON ATISHA DIPAMKARA SHRIJNANA'S
A Lamp for the Path to Enlightenment
AND LAMA JE TSONG KHAPA'S
Lines of Experience

Translated by
GESHE THUPTEN JINPA

Edited by
REBECCA McCLEN NOVICK,
THUPTEN JINPA AND NICHOLAS RIBUSH

Produced by the Lama Yeshe Wisdom Archive, Boston, Massachusetts
for Thubten Dhargye Ling Publications, Long Beach, California
www.tdling.com

First published 2002

20,000 copies for free distribution

THUBTEN DHARGYE LING
PO Box 90665
Long Beach
CA 90809, USA

ISBN 0-9623421-6-5

10 9 8 7 6 5 4 3 2 1

Cover photos by Don Farber
Book design by L.J.Sawlit

Printed in Canada on recycled, acid-free paper

CONTENTS

Publisher's Acknowledgments

THIS IS THE SECOND BOOK PUBLISHED by Thubten Dhargye Ling Publications for free distribution. We have been very gratified by the excellent response to our first, *Mirror of Wisdom*, by Venerable Geshe Tsultim Gyeltsen, our spiritual master and director, and feel sure that readers will enjoy *Illuminating the Path to Enlightenment*.

We are extremely grateful to His Holiness the Dalai Lama for accepting Geshe Gyeltsen's invitation to teach in Los Angeles in 2000, for choosing to offer us his commentaries on the profound texts, *A Lamp for the Path to Enlightenment*, by Atisha Dipamkara Shrijnana, and *Lines of Experience*, by Lama Tsong Khapa, and in particular, for giving us permission to publish this book for free distribution.

We also would like to express our gratitude to Geshe Thupten Jinpa for his expert translation during the teachings and for his work in reviewing the translation and his numerous editorial suggestions for improving the manuscript while it was in preparation.

We would also like to thank Rebecca McClen Novick and Dr. Nicholas Ribush for editing the book, Lisa Sawlit for designing it and the Lama Yeshe Wisdom Archive for supervising its production.

We extend heartfelt thanks to the many kind benefactors whose generous donations made this work possible. For major contributions, we thank in particular Doren and Mary Harper, John and Eleanor W. Allen, Richard Gere, Linda Bukowski, Hanh Nguyen and James N. Smith.

We are also most grateful to Randall Gates, Leslie Jamison, Lillie &

Stuart Scudder, Jeff Abrams, Chiyoko Aita, Mary Alexander, Janice Allen & Jim Davidson, Renee Allen, Nancy Andersen, Steve Anderson, Ruben Anton, Vicari Antonina, Diane April, Bettina Aptheker, Harvey Aronson, Deborah Arthur, Santina Aruta, Stephen Ascue, Darlene Ashley, Susan Augustson, Beatrice Avcollie, Babs Aydelott, Ikuko Bacon, Richard Baldwin, Christie Banks, Laura Baptista, Marguerite Barton & Vo-Thi-Cuc, Andrea Beardsley, Dory Beatrice, Captain Peter Beauclerk, Kathleen Becker, Yong Meng Beh, George Bekey, Alexa Bell, Nancy Bessette, Karen Blackwell, Michele Bohana, Vladamir Bojov, Sharon Bonney, Bernadette Boschert, Denise T. Bourque, Llance Bower, Fadhilla Bradley, Emilio Briceno, Don Broderson, Ross Brooke, Bonnie Brown, Lorraine Brown, Sergio Bruno, Kimoanh N. Bui, Ingrid Buraczenski, Danielle Cagaanan, Aryeri Calderon, Marsha Camblin, Anne Cannon, Alex Cao, Christina Huong Cao, Chuong Cao & Quynh M. Do, Julie Chang, Neil Chase, Robert Chase, Celia Chavez, Elizabeth Ann Chavez, Charng-Jui Chen, Jason Chen, Ling Chun Chen, Lotte Cherin, Herbert Chissell, Tenzin Chodron, Thubten Chodron, Florence P. Chotiner, Neil Christopherson, Barbara Clark, Eden Clearbrook, Michelle D. Coe, Colorado Mt. Zen Center, Horatio Costa, William Coulter, Dorothy Crompton, Hazel Crosbie, Kristin Crowell, Ruby Cubano, James Culnan, Dennis Cuocco, David Curtis, Frank Damavandi, Loan Kim Dang, Dung Phuong Dao, Tom Dawson, Jamie Delman, Brian M. Delrosario, Virgie Demanski, Yolanda De Silva, Trish Devitt, Theresa Dhondup, Camille N. Do, Janet Do, Kimberly Do, Ani Losang Dolma, Jeffrey Dreher, Marie C. Droney, Sheila Duddy, Ty Ebright, Elsa Echevarria, Laurence Eggers, Pamela Eiselman, Jacalyn Elder, Elizabeth Ennis, Kaye Eshnaur, Suzanne Esnard, Stella Estes, Robert Evans, Steven Evans, Steven Everton, Erin Farber, John Feldmann, Christine Ferrero, George Fields, Susan Fischer, Carla Fisher, Patricia Fitzgerald, Karen Flanders, Catherine Flanigan, Tapas Fleming, Christina Flynn, Stefanie Foote, Kelli Fortenbaugh,

Paula Fouce, Corinne Fowler, Jim Fowler, Robert Friedman, Darlene Fung, Laura Gasparrini, Bill Gau, Benjamin M. Gee, Bill Glaser, Amanda Glosgow, Gary Goldman, Maximilian Graenitz, Jeffrey Griffin, Eric Gruenwald, Ellen Gurian, Gail Gustafson, Virginia G. Gutierrel, Robert Gworek, Krysia Haber, Rose Haig, Cheryl Hamada, Kimberly Harding, Nadia Marie Harding, Victoria Hargreaves, Lynda Harkness, Robin Hart, Aurora Hassett, John Hatherley, William Haynes, Midge Henline, Janet Hewins, Thao X. Ho, Thuy Vinh Ho, Leeann Hoa, Barbara Hodgson & Brian Nishikawa, J. Hoffman, Kathleen Hoffman, Martha Holsclaw, Ngai Kong Hong, Vicki Hons, Reginald Horne, Cynthia Houck, Adrienne House, James Houston, Clay Howard, Susan Howard, Matthew Howatt, Ron Howlett, Bella Hui, Sharon Hurley, Angela Igrisan, Institute of Buddhist Dialectics, Elaine Jackson, Sonia Jacobs, Yunching Jan, Karen Jefchak, Rebecca Jeffs, Osel Jason, Mary Johnson, Jeff Jones, Nigel Jones, Fred Ju, Alex Juncosa, Sri Mewaty Jusuf, Ani Tenzin Kacho, Peter Tamam Kahn, Jacobo Kamar, Trisha & Paul Kane, Kelly Kanika-Enn, Judy Kann, Gary Kazanjian, Myoshin Kelley, Peter Kemble, Ellie Kierson, Sylvia Kimbel, Brian Kistler, Rodney Kizziah, Barbara Knapp, Kevin Knapp, Gustav Koehler, Kathleen Koehn, Lisa Koritsoglou, Alexis Krasilovsky, James Kromwall, Angel La Canfora, Suzanne La Pierre, Laurie Lai, Cyndie Lam, Katherine Lambert, Marina De Bellagente LaPalma, Helen Lau, Lance Layton, Duyen Le, Hoai Xuan Le, Winnie Le, Barbara Lee, Stanlie Lee, Charles Lewis, Kenneth Liberman, Lisa Liebman, Mari Lineberry, Dunja Lingwood, Linzer, Diana Lion, Tseng-Ping Liu, Rosaura Loarca, Gary Longenecker, Jairo Lopez, Mai T. Luong, Barbara MacGowan, Hong Thanh Mai, Christel Maiwald, Vicky Manchester, Stephanie Manzo, Bertha Marcil, Carol Marcil, Osa Marell, Barry J. Marks, Dawn Martin, Kamran Mashayekh, David Mastrandrea, Leigh Matthes, Roosevelt & Patricia Matthews, Tracy Mays, Troy McAuley, Elizabeth A. McBride, Michael McClure, Caroline McEwen, John McGinness,

Bernard McGrane, Susan McKelvey, Nola Lee McNally, Judith McReynolds-Yantis, Men-Tsee-Khang, Georgia Metz, George Miller, Maryanne Miss, Radmila Moacanin, Sally A. Molini, Judith Montgomery, Bonnie Moore, J. Moore, Rebecca Morales, David Morgan, Jane Morrison, Louis Muchy, Mudra Inc., Karen Mueller, Marcy Muray, Tiffany Murray, Namgyal Monastery, Narayana, Erma Nelson, Lisa Neuweld, Kham Ngo, Kim Ngo, Che & Dolma Ngokhang, Duc Tam Nguyen, Dung Anh Nguyen, Tam Nguyen, Xung Dao Nguyen, Yen Nguyen, Rosanne Nicassio, Linda Nichols, Randy Niebergall, Daniel Nielsen, Pua Laa Norwood, Tenzing Nuba, Terrie Nugen, Dr. Dickey Nyeronsha, Sean B. O'Byrne, Andre Orianne, Chris Paggi, Sasha Alexander Panov, Martin Parks, Janet Parrish, Penny Paster, Michele Paterson, Janet Pearson, Bob Pannetta, Li Ann Pfeiffer, Duc Dinh Pham, Ha Ngoc Pham, Mai & Quan Pham, Chi Thi Ngoc Phan, Tseten Phanucharas, Robert Phipps, Khanh T. Phung, Carol-Renee Pierpoint, Margaret Pilcher, Rick Pinson, Pam A. Porcaro, Ellen Powell, Richard Prinz & Beverly Gwyn, Lee Purser, Grace Quach, Hung Quach & Tam-minh Nguyen, Linda Quakenbush, Chan Cuong Quan, Romy Ragan, Mary Ann Ramey, Margaret Randall, William Rauch, Barbara R. Reber, April Reeder, Faryl Saliman Reingold, Arlene Reiss, Sherilyn Renstrom, Edward Rice, Terry Richardson, Norma Rockman, Sheila Rollins, Roberta Rolnick, Alex Roman, Shirley Rose, George M. Rosenberg, Dan Roules, Suzanne Royce, Carol Royce-Wilder, Alice Runge, John W. Russell, Dika Ryan, Jaret Sacrey, Janet Sanders, Sanghapala Foundation, Robert Sant, Inge Santoso, Robert Saunders, Lynn Scalzi, Julie Scarzi, K.B. Schaetzel Hill, L.J. Schaetzel-Hill, Robert Schafer, Christine Schneider, Butch Schuman, David & Susan Schwartz, Deborah Schwartz, Skip Shaputnik, Gail Shatsky, Andrew Shaw, Richard Shea, Allyson Shelly, Beverly Sherman, James Silberstein, Casey Silvey, Diana Simons, Mr. or Ms. Simpson, Claudia Smelser, Margo Smith, Scott Snibbe, Victoria Snowdon, Lynne Sonenberg,

Edmund Spaeth, Wayne Speeds, Danleigh Spievak, Jeff Stankiewicz, Diana Stark, Cary Steen, Bill Stefanek, Regula Stewart, Phillip Stokes, David Studhalter, David & Susan Stumpf, Preston Sult, Connie Sun, Iris Swallow, Darren Swimmer, Valeryie Szymanski, Sara Taft, Robert J. Talbert, Betty Tallarida, Charlotte Tang, An Tao, Sandra Tatlock, Ellen Taylor, Christina Tedesco, Francine Thomas, Richard Thompson, Susan Thurben, Jo Ann Tirado, Michele Trahan, Thanh Tram & Mai T. Nguyen, Daniele Tran, Dinh Thang Tran, Oanh Hoang Tran, Xuan Tran, Tse Chen Ling Center, Christien Tuttle, David Uyekawa, Wilhelmina Van De Poll, D. Varano, Douglas Varchol, Leopoldo Villela, Ted Viramonte, Tony Vitale, Kim Vo, Nathan Vo, Quince K. Vo, Alicia H. Vogel (Ani Lhundub Jampa), Lynn Wade, Cynthia Walgampaya, Judyth Weaver, Patrick Weaver, Sean Weber-Small, Kenneth Weed, Nick Weeks, Katherine Wehde, John Western, Ralph Westrum, Laurren B. Whistler, Jami Whitelaw, Catherine Whyte, Emese Williams, Carol Wilson Ttee, Victoria Witherow, Siewfan Wong, Jessie Wood, Marta Woodhull, Key Wu, Peggy P. Wu, Susan Wyss, Y.P., Cynthia Yellowhair, Jigme Yugay, Anna Zack, Michela Zanchi, Angela Zaragoza, Renee Zepezauer, Vicki Zimmerman and Elizabeth Zographos.

We are also deeply grateful to the many benefactors who asked to remain anonymous and to those kind people whose contributions were received after the book went to press. Thank you all so much.

Last but not least, we offer sincere thanks to Lara Brooke for her tireless work for the Center and to all the other students of Thubten Dhargye Ling and our other centers as well, for their devotion to and constant support of our kind teacher, Geshe Tsultim Gyeltsen, and his far-reaching Dharma work.

FOREWORD

WE AT THUBTEN DHARGYE LING are very happy for the opportunity to present His Holiness the Dalai Lama's *lam-rim* teachings in book form. Due to changing times and circumstances, more and more people in the West are taking a serious interest in Buddhism, or Dharma. It is for this reason that when His Holiness visited Los Angeles in 1997 to teach on Nagarjuna's *Precious Garland,* I requested that he return in 2000 to give a teaching on the lam-rim. His Holiness accepted this request very happily. I did not ask for His Holiness to teach a specific lam-rim text, but out of his deep insight and altruism, he decided to combine two lam-rim texts—Atisha's *Lamp for the Path to Enlightenment* and Lama Tsong Khapa's concise lam-rim, *Lines of Experience.*

Buddhism originated from its founding teacher, Shakyamuni Buddha, who gave 84,000 forms of teaching. Lam-rim means "stages of the path to enlightenment." It was the great Indian master, Atisha, who wrote the first lam-rim text, *A Lamp for the Path to Enlightenment,* which condenses all 84,000 teachings into a single body of work. Atisha wrote this text in Tibet at the request of a Tibetan king. He then sent the text to India, where all the great realized scholars and *mahasiddhas* received it with praise and appreciation. It must be due to the good fortune and merit of the Tibetan people, they said, that Atisha had composed such a wonderful text.

Atisha's lam-rim text is very brief but extremely profound, and Lama Tsong Khapa knew that without some further explanation, many people would not be able to understand everything that it contained. Taking Atisha's lam-rim as the root text, Lama Tsong Khapa elucidated the teachings in three different versions: the *Great Lam-rim,* the

Middling Lam-rim and the *Short Lam-rim.*

I believe that His Holiness the Dalai Lama has very deep reasons for giving these lam-rim teachings. Many of us wish to practice the tantric path with the sincere hope of achieving complete enlightenment as soon as possible. For us to become completely enlightened through the practice of tantra, however, there are some essential preliminaries that we need to practice first. To be truly qualified to practice tantra, we need to cultivate the three principal paths—renunciation, *bodhicitta* (the altruistic mind of enlightenment) and the wisdom realizing emptiness. The lam-rim teachings cover all these subjects in great detail.

If we cannot achieve realization of these paths before engaging in tantra, we should at least have familiarized our mind with them and gained some experience in their practice. In this respect, the lam-rim teachings are indispensable guides. We find explanations of the three principal paths throughout all the Buddha's teachings but what the lam-rim does is to present them in a manner that is relatively easy to comprehend and practice.

Whenever His Holiness the Dalai Lama gives a public teaching, he presents the text in a very skillful way that meets the needs of people and practitioners at all levels. This lam-rim teaching is no exception. It is my belief that by reading the profound yet easy to follow commentary in this publication, many practitioners will receive tremendous benefit. Because of the depth of His Holiness the Dalai Lama's spiritual experiences and realizations, as well as his skillful methods and infinite compassion and wisdom, his teachings are unsurpassed by any other. In order to preserve these invaluable teachings, not only for the present generation but for all future ones, we at Thubten Dhargye Ling are making every effort to ensure that they are available to the public in the form of videotapes, audiotapes and books.

I would very much like to encourage readers to read this lam-rim commentary over and over again. With each reading and contemplation, you will gain deeper insight into these teachings and find better ways to apply them to your own mental development. In Buddhism, we talk about cultivating three types of wisdom; those arising through listening to teachings, contemplating their meaning and meditating on the ascertained meaning.

These three types of wisdom have to arise sequentially in our mind stream. Through listening to teachings, we gain understanding; through contemplation, we deepen this understanding; through meditation, we apply the teachings to ourselves—in other words, we engage in the practice. We are very fortunate to have this wonderful human life and the opportunity to study and practice these teachings. We should make our best efforts, therefore, to follow the Dharma so that we will experience the benefits not only in this lifetime but also in many future lifetimes—and not just for ourselves but for other sentient beings as well.

We at Thubten Dhargye Ling hope that through contemplating and meditating on these teachings, readers will gain great spiritual benefit. We hope that this publication will facilitate greater intimacy with the three principal paths of renunciation, altruism and the wisdom of emptiness. May we all be able to cultivate these paths within our own minds.

We dedicate the virtue arising from this publication to the long life of His Holiness the Dalai Lama and all other great spiritual masters who uphold the pure teachings of the Buddha for the benefit of others.

May this world be free of sickness, starvation, warfare and weapons of mass destruction. May we all be able to accumulate the necessary facilities for our own well-being and for the attainment of peace in the world, and may we develop the ability to extend our affection and love beyond ourselves so that we can all learn to help and care for one another better.

Geshe Tsultim Gyeltsen

Spiritual Master and Director
Thubten Dhargye Ling, Tibetan Monastery
Long Beach, California, USA

UNIVERSAL RESPONSIBILITY

DEAR BROTHERS AND SISTERS, I am very happy to be here with you. I always believe that we human beings are all essentially the same—mentally, emotionally and physically. Of course, there are minor differences, such as shape and color, but we all have two eyes, two ears and one nose. Therefore, I am always happy to interact with and talk to my fellow human brothers and sisters. In this way, I learn new things, mainly when I receive a question on something entirely unexpected. Audience members come up with new concepts or points, which gives me the opportunity to reflect and analyze. It's very useful.

I want to make clear, however—perhaps even warn you—that you should not expect too much. There are no miracles. I am very skeptical of such things. It is very dangerous if people come to my talks believing that the Dalai Lama has some kind of healing power, for example. I myself doubt those who claim to have the power to heal. Some time ago, at a large gathering in England, I said the same thing. At that time I told the audience that if there is a real healer out there, I want to show that person my skin problems. Sometimes it can be quite pleasant to scratch the itch, but as the Indian Buddhist master Nagarjuna said, "It's better not to have the itching than to have the pleasure of scratching." Anyway, so far, I have never met such a person. However, if you are here simply out of curiosity, that's perfectly fine. I'm very happy to have this opportunity to talk to you and would also like to express my deep appreciation to those who have organized this event.

The fundamental thing is that everyone wants a happy, successful life. This is not only our goal but our legitimate right as well. The question then arises, how do we achieve this happy life? It seems that in these modern times, when technology and material facilities are so well developed and freely available, we get the idea that material things are the ultimate factor in the satisfaction of our desires and the fulfillment of our goals. Thus, we have too much expectation of material things and put too much trust in them; our strong materialistic beliefs give us false hope in that which truly lacks a firm basis. As a result, we neglect our inner values and state of mind.

By relying so much on external things to make our lives meaningful, we move further away from basic human values. Of course, material development is essential and very useful, but it is wrong to expect that all our problems can be solved through external means. When material and spiritual development are combined, however, we can achieve our goal of a happy life. Therefore, while focusing on material development, it is essential that we pay attention to inner values as well.

When I use the word "spiritual," I don't necessarily mean religious faith. It is quite obvious that there are two levels of spirituality—spirituality with religious faith and that without. Obviously, an individual can manage to lead a meaningful life without religious faith, but you can't be a happy person without the spirituality of basic human values. As long as we remain human, there is no way that we can neglect this.

What are these basic human values? There are two levels. On one level, there is the sense of caring for one another, sharing with one another—the sense of oneness that comes from seeing all people as brothers and sisters in a single human family, bringing respect, tolerance and self-discipline. We even find some of these qualities in the animal kingdom. However, on another level, because of our human intelligence and understanding of far-reaching consequences, we can deliberately increase certain qualities and try to restrain others. In this way, humans are much more sophisticated than animals.

Human beings and animals equally have the same basic desire for happiness or satisfaction. This is common to all sentient beings. The unique thing about us, however, is our *intelligence.* The desire to attain happiness, pleasure and satisfaction mainly through the five senses is not a uniquely human thing; there is not much to distinguish us from animals in this regard. What does distinguish us from animals, however, is our ability to use our faculty of intelligence in our quest to fulfill our natural desire to be happy and overcome suffering. It is this ability to judge between the long- and short-term consequences of our behavior and actions that really distinguishes us from animals; utilizing our unique human qualities in the right way is what proves us to be true human beings.

Another important factor is that there are two kinds of pain and pleasure—pain and pleasure on the physical, or sensory, level and those on the mental level. If we examine our daily lives, it will become clear that we can subdue physical pain mentally. When we are happy and calm, we can easily ignore physical discomfort, such as pain and unpleasant sensations. When, however, we are unhappy or disturbed, then even the best of external factors, such as good companions, money and fame, cannot make us happy. This suggests that no matter how powerful our sensory experiences might be, they cannot overwhelm our state of mind; mental experience is superior to physical. It is in this mental realm of happiness and suffering or pain and pleasure that the application of human intelligence plays a tremendously influential role.

Human intelligence itself is neutral; it is just an instrument that can be utilized in either destructive or constructive ways. For example, many of our sufferings come about as the result of the power of our imagination and ability to think about the future, which can create doubt, expectation, disappointment and fear. Animals don't have these problems. If an animal finds good food and shelter and there are no immediate disturbances, it can exist quite peacefully, but even when we human beings are well fed and surrounded by good companions, nice music and so forth, our sophistication and expectations don't allow us to relax. Human intelligence, in other words, is a source of worry and problems. The unhappiness that arises from an overactive imagination cannot be resolved by material means.

Human intelligence, therefore, can be very influential either negatively or positively. The key factor in directing it more positively is having the right mental attitude. To have a happy life—happy days and happy nights—it is extremely important to combine our human intelligence with basic human values. If our minds are peaceful, open and calm during the day, our dreams will reflect these experiences and be happy. If during the day we experience fear, agitation and doubt, we will continue to encounter troubles in our dreams. Therefore, to have happiness twenty-four hours a day, we must have the right mental attitude.

Instead of thinking about money and material things every minute of the day, we should pay more attention to our inner world. It is interesting to ask ourselves such questions as, "Who am I?" and "Where is my I?" Usually, we take our "I" for granted. We feel that within us there is something solid and independent that is the owner of our mind, body and possessions; if we reflect on and examine where this so-called powerful and precious self actually resides, it will prove to be quite useful. We should also ask, "What is the mind? Where is it?" because the greatest of all disturbing forces are the negative emotions. When these destructive emotions are fully developed, we become their slave; as if mad. Therefore, when negative emotions arise, it is useful to inquire, "Where does all this come from?"

The key factor in developing and increasing basic human values—the sense of caring for and sharing with one another—is human affection, a feeling of closeness with one another. This quality is present within us from the moment of our conception. According to some medical scientists, the unborn child can recognize its mother's voice. This indicates that even then, the child feels close to and dear towards its mother. Once the child is born, he or she spontaneously sucks its mother's milk. The mother also experiences a feeling of closeness to her child. Because of this, her milk flows freely. If either side lacked that feeling of intimacy, the child would not survive. Each of us started our life that way and without human affection would definitely not have survived.

Medical science also teaches us that emotions play a very important role in health. Fear and hatred, for example, are very bad for us. Also, when negative emotions arise strongly, certain parts of our brain become blocked and our intelligence cannot function properly. We can see from our daily experience as well that strong negative emotions can make us uncomfortable and tense, leading to problems with digestion and sleep and causing some of us to resort to tranquilizers, sleeping pills, alcohol or other drugs.

Furthermore, when certain negative emotions develop they can disturb our body's natural balance, resulting in high blood pressure and other kinds of disease. One medical researcher presented data at a conference showing that people who frequently use words such as "I," "me" and "mine" have a greater risk of heart attack. Thus, it seems that if you want to have a heart attack, you should repeat these words like a mantra and all the time say, "I, I, I, I, I, I."

If we think of ourselves as very precious and absolute, our whole mental focus becomes very narrow and limited and even minor problems can seem unbearable. If, however, we can think more holistically and see our problems from a broader perspective, they will become insignificant. For example, if we switch our mental attitude from concern for our own welfare to that of others, our mind automatically widens and our own problems appear much less important and easier to face.

The actual beneficiary of the practice of compassion and caring for others is oneself. We may have the impression that the main beneficiaries of the practice of compassion are those on the receiving end; that the practice of compassion is relevant only for those concerned about others and irrelevant for those who are not, because its main benefit goes to others. This is a mistake. The immediate benefit of practicing compassion is actually experienced by the practitioner.

Because our mind broadens and we feel more comfortable when we think about humanity and the welfare of others, if we can generate this kind of mental attitude, whenever we meet someone, we will feel that here is another human brother or sister and will immediately be able to communicate with ease. When we think only about ourselves, our inner door remains closed and we find it very difficult to communicate with our fellow human beings.

The practice of compassion and caring for others immediately brings us inner strength and inner peace. Of course, compassion may also benefit others indirectly, but what is certain is the benefit that we ourselves experience. It is quite clear, therefore, that if we are really concerned about our own future and the happiness of our own life, we should develop a mental attitude in which the practice of compassion plays a central role. I sometimes jokingly tell people that if we want to be truly selfish, then we should be wisely selfish rather than foolishly selfish.

This is the reality. Think about these points and experiment with them. Eventually you will develop greater awareness of what I'm talking about.

I am a sixty-four year old Buddhist monk and in a few days I will be sixty-five. The greater part of my life has not been happy. Most people already know about my difficult experiences. When I was fifteen I lost my freedom; at the age of twenty-four I lost my country. Now, forty-one years have passed since I became a refugee and news from my homeland is always very saddening. Yet inside, my mental state seems quite peaceful. Bad news tends to go in one ear and out the other; not much remains stuck within my mind. The result is that my peace of mind is not too disturbed.

This is not because I'm some kind of special person. I joke with my Chinese friends about the Chinese term *huo-fo*, which means "living buddha." The very term itself is dangerous; it's completely wrong. The Tibetan word is "lama"; in Sanskrit, it's "guru." There's no hint of "living buddha" in these words, so I have no idea how the Chinese got "living buddha" out of them. Anyway, whether people call me a living buddha, a god-king or, in some cases, a devil or counter-revolutionary, it doesn't matter. The reality is that I'm just a human being; a simple Buddhist monk. There are no differences between us, and according to my own experience, if we pay more attention to our inner world then our lives can be happier. You can achieve many things as a result of living in a materially developed society, but if, in addition, you pay more attention to your inner world, your life will become much richer and more complete.

There are many parts of the world where whole communities are still struggling to achieve basic living standards. When people have to fight for their daily sustenance, almost all of their energy and concentration needs to be directed towards that end, which does not really allow anxiety and mental problems to come to the surface. By contrast, there is less of a struggle for daily survival in the more affluent Northern countries because these societies have reached a relatively high level of material development. This, however, gives people there the opportunity to pay attention to problems that are more emotional and mental in nature.

Through training our minds we can become more peaceful. This will give us greater opportunities for creating the peaceful families and human communities that are the foundation of world peace. With inner strength, we can face problems on the familial, societal and even global levels in a more realistic way. Non-violence does not mean passivity. We need to solve problems through dialogue in a spirit of reconciliation. This is the real meaning of non-violence and the source of world peace.

This approach can also be very useful in ecology. We always hear about a better environment, world peace, non-violence and so forth, but such goals are not achieved through the application of regulations or United Nations resolutions; it takes individual transformation. Once we have developed a peaceful society in which problems are negotiated through dialogue, we can seriously think about demilitarization—first on the national level; then on the regional level; and finally, on the global level. However, it will be very difficult to achieve these things unless individuals themselves undergo a change within their own minds.

QUESTION AND ANSWER PERIOD

Question. What can Americans do to counteract the violence that is so prevalent in our society?

His Holiness. I think I just answered that! Otherwise, I have no special answer to your question. However, transforming our mental attitude is our main task. How can we accomplish that? How can we carry that work into the family and school? Here, education is essential. Not through prayer or religious meditation and so forth but through proper education. The various levels of educational institution have a very important role to play in the promotion of the human spirit in the form of secular ethics. I'm not an educator, but people need to talk more seriously about how to improve and expand the educational curriculum to make it more complete. The media can also play an important role in the promotion of human values. Otherwise, I'm not sure what can be done.

Question. In this materialistic and consumer-driven society, how does one overcome the desire for and attachment to material goods?

His Holiness. If you think deeply in terms of the spiritual practice of cultivating modest desires and contentment, I would say that in some respects there are more opportunities for people living in materially affluent societies. People in less materially developed societies haven't had the opportunity to really experience the limitations of material conditions and facilities. If you live in a materially affluent society, it is easier for you to see the limits of material facilities in terms of providing satisfaction. So I would say that in a materially enriched society, there are, in fact, more opportunities for spiritual practice. Of course, it all depends upon the individual's own attitudes and thoughts.

However, this deeply embedded idea of the West being a consumer-driven, materialistic culture may contain an element of imagination. People make these categorical differences between Eastern and Western cultures and then, as Westerners, you start to believe in them. You think that your lives are driven by materialistic values; you project a certain image of your own culture and begin to believe in it, perpetuating a certain mindset.

Among my Western friends, I know individuals with a tremendous commitment and dedication to the practice of Buddhadharma. They also have quite a high degree of experience based on prolonged meditative practices and live according to the experiences they have gained. We can find such people in both the East and the West. The basic nature of all human beings is the same.

Question. Lately, many Americans have become dependent on anti-depressant drugs. To some it is a serious medical concern but to others it may be just an easy way out. What is Your Holiness's opinion on this question?

His Holiness. When we talk about medication such as anti-depressant drugs, of course there are different conditions. In some cases, depression may be caused by physiological or biological conditions due to imbalances within the body. Under such circumstances, using an anti-depressant drug can actually help the individual and is an effective way of handling that medical problem. However, there may be other instances where the mental distress or depression does not have a biological basis but comes from psychological factors. It is then more effective to rely on internal methods such as mind training or meditation.

As to the question of people using anti-depressant drugs simply as a way of gaining some kind of relaxation or some kind of easy way out, that's clearly an abuse of the substance. The relief that individuals get from using drugs in this way is only temporary. While the drug retains its potency in the body, the person remains in a pleasurable state, but the moment it loses its potency, the person is back to where he or she was before. Therefore, it is more effective to rely on internal techniques. With these, you can later recall the relief you gained as a result of your meditation and the relief itself will last longer.

Question. How would you recommend that Americans practice Buddhism if they feel called to it, without adopting the Tibetan culture as well?

His Holiness. This is definitely possible. There is nothing uniquely Tibetan about the Four Noble Truths, for example. Fundamentally, there is no particular reference to Tibetan or Indian culture in Tibetan Buddhism. It is not about East or West.

Question. At the moment of death, how can a layperson remain in peace instead of fear?

His Holiness. As I mentioned earlier, if you are calm and peaceful during the day, your dreams will also be calm and peaceful. By extension, if your day-to-day life is peaceful and friendly, so too will be your death. That's the best preparation for a peaceful death. If your life is filled with cruelty, fear and hatred, you will find it very difficult to die in peace.

As a Buddhist monk, I believe that there is a next life. The Buddhist practice of tantra, in particular, contains many unique preparations for death and it is very important for practitioners to familiarize ourselves with them so that we can actualize these practices when we die. Therefore, in my daily practice, I meditate on my own death and rebirth repeatedly. This is supposed to prepare me for death, but I'm still not sure whether or not I'll be equipped to handle it when it actually comes. Sometimes I feel that when it does, I might start getting excited about whether or not I'll be able to implement these practices effectively.

Question. Now that Communism has been discredited, how can we control the growing gap between rich and poor?

His Holiness. This is a really important question. Everybody can see that on the global level there is a huge gap between the rich nations and the poor; we find a similar divide within individual countries as well. In America, for example, the number of billionaires is increasing, while the poor remain poor and in some cases get even poorer. Just the other day, I met an old friend who told me about the work she is doing in Washington DC. She said that the living conditions of some of the families she has visited are so desperate that they are unsuitable for any human being to live in. While she was explaining her experiences, she began to cry, and I also felt very moved.

This is not only morally wrong but also impractical. We have to think seriously about how to reduce this problem. I've heard that a number of affluent families are now willing to share some of their wealth.

Last year, some friends in Chicago told me that some of the wealthier families now have more courage to share. This is good news; the more we develop this compassionate attitude, the more we can diminish the gap between rich and poor.

On a global level, however, I feel that the initiative must come from the poorer countries, largely through education. During recent visits to South Africa and other African countries, I found a great divide between the elite and the masses and that many poor people lacked self-confidence. It is very important for the poor to make an effort to transform their mental attitude through education. The wealthy can assist them in this by providing educational and training facilities and equipment.

This, then, leads us to the question of population. There are now more than six billion human beings on this planet. This is an extremely serious matter. If we try to raise the standard of living of the poor and undeveloped countries to that of countries in the Northern hemisphere, it's questionable whether the world's natural resources will be sufficient for everybody. Problems such as this are caused by a lack of awareness and a failure to use human intelligence properly. All countries, but poor ones in particular, tend to look only at immediate problems instead of thinking long-term. Nevertheless, through education, solutions will eventually be found.

Question. Your Holiness, with so many wars being declared in the name of religion, can you explain why Tibet has not taken a more violent approach towards attaining freedom?

His Holiness. First, I believe that humans are basically kind and gentle and that the use of violence goes against our fundamental nature. Second, it is difficult to find in human history examples of military solutions leading to lasting resolution of whatever the problem was. Furthermore, these days, national boundaries are becoming less important; for example, in the modern economy, there are basically none. Moreover, information technology and tourism are turning the world into a single human community. Therefore, the concept of independence has less meaning these days.

Things are highly interdependent. The very concepts of "we" and "they" are becoming irrelevant. War is out of date because our neighbors are part of ourselves. We see this in economic, educational and environmental issues. Although we may have some ideological differences or other conflicts with our neighbor, economically and environmentally we share essentially the same country, and destroying our neighbor is destroying ourselves. It's foolish.

Take Kosovo, for example. America's military campaign was seen as some kind of liberation on humanitarian grounds entailing the use of limited force. Perhaps the motivation was good and the goal also justified, but because of the use of violence, instead of hatred being reduced, in some cases it might have increased. Right from the beginning, I personally had reservations about the use of force in that situation, despite the positive motivation and goal. Basically, violence is obsolete.

In the case of Tibet, whether we like it or not, we have to live side by side with our Chinese brothers and sisters. Tibetans have had relations with China for almost two thousand years. Sometimes they have been happy; sometimes not. Right now we're going through an unhappy period, but regardless of this, we still have to live together as neighbors. Therefore, in order to live peacefully, harmoniously and with friendship in future, it is extremely important that while carrying on our struggle for freedom, we avoid using violence. This is my fundamental belief.

Another thing is that to find a solution to the problems between China and Tibet, the support of the Chinese public is essential. There is growing support and solidarity for the Tibetan cause among Chinese people and this is very encouraging. But if we resort to violence and

cause Chinese people to shed blood, even those Chinese who intellectu-
ally recognize that Tibet's struggle is just and that the Tibetan people
have really suffered during the so-called peaceful liberation of Tibet will
withdraw their support because their own brothers and sisters are suffering. Therefore, it is extremely important that throughout our struggle we continue to rely on non-violent means.

Question. How does someone maintain a spiritual diet or spiritual nour-
ishment in such a busy world? Is there a very quick and simple mantra
one can say when first arising or something to focus on during the day
to feel calm?

His Holiness. You can do this through training your mind. Start by getting up early in the morning. The late Thomas Merton, a Trappist
monk, got up at 2:30 in the morning and went to bed at 7:30 in the
evening. My schedule begins one hour later; I get up at 3:30 and go to
bed at 8:30. So, you need to be able to sacrifice staying up late and
nightclubbing. If you really enjoy that, maybe you can do it once a
month.

   Then, getting up early, examine your daily life and some of the
points that I have already mentioned. Examine and analyze. This is the
proper way; I don't know any simpler method. Furthermore, I'm very
skeptical of those who claim that problems can be solved just by closing
your eyes. Problems can be solved only through developing your mental
attitude properly, which takes time and effort.

Question. You spend every moment dedicated to others. If you could
take a vacation for yourself alone, what would you do?

His Holiness. I would have a long sleep! The other day, I arrived in
Washington DC from India. It's a very long flight and I was exhausted.

I went to sleep around 5:30 p.m. and woke up the next morning around 4:30 a.m.—I slept more than eleven hours. I found it very useful. So, if I do take a vacation, I'll have a ten-hour sleep. Then, of course, in my daily life, meditation is also a method for relaxation. In meditation, we think about and analyze life, mind and self. If your analytical meditation goes well, you feel relaxed; if it doesn't, you just get more tired.

Question. What single action can each of us take to demonstrate universal responsibility?

His Holiness. One thing that we all can do as individuals is to ensure that our concerns for the environment become a part of our lives. I myself never take a bath; just a shower. Baths waste a lot of water; in many parts of the world, there's a serious shortage of drinking water. It's also important to conserve electricity. Whenever I leave a room, I switch off the light. This has become so much a part of my life that I do it without conscious thought. Such actions are part of my own small contribution to the environment.

1

GENERAL INTRODUCTION

STUDYING THESE TEACHINGS is a bit like doing construction work upon our mind. This kind of work is not always easy, but some of its aspects make it less difficult. For example, we don't need money, laborers, technicians or technology. Everything we require is already there, within our mind. Therefore, with the right kind of effort and awareness, mental development can be easy.

I sometimes feel a little hesitant about giving Buddhist teachings in the West, because I think that it is better and safer for people to stay within their own religious tradition. But out of the millions of people who live in the West, naturally there will be some who find the Buddhist approach more effective or suitable. Even among Tibetans, there are those who practice Islam instead of Buddhism. If you do adopt Buddhism as your religion, however, you must still maintain an appreciation for the other major religious traditions. Even if they no longer work for you, millions of other people have received immense benefit from them in the past and continue to do so. Therefore, it is important for you to respect them.

The teachings we are studying here are based on two texts: *A Lamp for the Path to Enlightenment* [Tib: *Jang-chub lam-gyi drön-ma*] by the Indian master, Atisha Dipamkara Shrijnana,[1] and *Lines of Experience* [Tib: *Lam-rim nyam-gur* or *Lam-rim nyam-len dor-du*], by Lama Tsong Khapa.

The skillful and compassionate Shakyamuni Buddha taught diverse types of Buddhadharma within a collection of 84,000 scriptures for the diverse mental dispositions and spiritual inclinations of his listeners. The essence of all these teachings is presented in such excellent treatises as Atisha's *Lamp for the Path*, which presents the systematic approach of an individual on the path to enlightenment.

With this as a basis, Lama Tsong Khapa composed three versions of lam-rim texts: an extensive version known as the *Great Exposition of the Path to Enlightenment*,[2] a medium-length version known as the *Middling Exposition of the Stages of the Path;* and the text we are studying here, the *Short Exposition of the Stages of the Path*, which is also called *Lines of Experience* or *Songs of Spiritual Experience.*

Although I am the one explaining the texts we'll be studying here, you don't necessarily have to see me as your spiritual teacher. Instead, you can take my explanations to heart by relating to me more as a spiritual friend or colleague. Furthermore, don't simply believe what I say without question, but use it as a basis for personal reflection and, in that way, develop your understanding of the Dharma.

Whenever we engage in teaching, studying or listening to the Buddhadharma, it is very important to ensure that we adopt the correct motivation and attitude within our hearts and minds. We do this by taking refuge in the Three Jewels (Buddha, Dharma and Sangha) and reaffirming our generation of the mind of enlightenment (the altruistic intention) through reciting the following verse three times:

> I take refuge until I am enlightened
> In the Buddha, the Dharma and the Sangha.
> By the positive potential I generate
> Through studying these teachings,
> May I attain buddhahood for the benefit of all.

It is also traditional at the beginning of a teaching to recite verses making salutations to the Buddha, such as those that appear in Nagarjuna's text, *Fundamentals of the Middle Way*. At the conclusion of this text, there is a verse that states, "I salute the Buddha who revealed the path that pacifies all suffering." The Buddha presented the path that pacifies all suffering in the following way.

Since the sufferings we all wish to avoid result from fundamentally mistaken ways of viewing the world, the way we eliminate them is by cultivating a correct understanding of the nature of reality. Therefore, in this verse, Nagarjuna salutes the Buddha for revealing the path that shows us how to cultivate a correct understanding of the nature of reality.

THE PURPOSE OF DHARMA PRACTICE

What is the purpose of the Dharma? Just like other spiritual traditions, Buddhadharma is an instrument for training the mind—something we use to try to work out the problems that we all experience; problems that originate mainly at the mental level. Negative emotional forces create mental unrest, such as unhappiness, fear, doubt, frustration and so forth; these negative mental states then cause us to engage in negative activities, which in turn bring us more problems and more suffering. Practicing Dharma is a way of working out these problems, be they long-term or immediate. In other words, Dharma protects us from unwanted suffering.

Buddhadharma means bringing discipline and inner tranquility into our mind. Therefore, when we talk about transforming our mind and developing inner qualities, the only way we can do this is to utilize the mind itself. There is nothing else we can use to bring about such change.

Thus, we should realize that much of what we do not desire— unwanted events, unhappiness and suffering—actually comes about as a result of our mistaken way of viewing the world and our destructive thoughts and emotions. These negative minds create both immediate unhappiness and future suffering as well.

Underlying all of this is a fundamental ignorance, a fundamentally flawed way of perceiving reality. In Buddhism, this is called "self-grasping," or "grasping at self-existence." Since this is the case, the way to eliminate negative aspects of mind and the suffering they create is to see through the delusion of these mental processes and cultivate their opponent—the wisdom that is correct insight into the ultimate nature of reality. Through cultivating this insight and applying it as an antidote, we will be able to dispel the suffering and undesirable events in our lives.

To succeed in this, we must first recognize what the negative and positive aspects of mind are and be able to distinguish between them. Once we develop a clear understanding of the negative aspects of mind and their destructive potential, the wish to distance ourselves from them will arise naturally within us. Similarly, when we recognize the positive aspects of mind and their potential benefit, we will naturally aspire to gain and enhance these mental qualities. Such transformation of mind cannot be imposed on us from the outside but happens only on the basis of voluntary acceptance and great enthusiasm inspired by a clear awareness of the benefits to be gained.

Time is always moving, minute-by-minute and second-by-second. As time moves on, so do our lives. Nobody can stop this movement. However, one thing is in our own hands, and that is whether or not we waste the time that we have; whether we use it in a negative way or a constructive way. The passage of time through which we live our lives is the same for all of us and there is also a basic equality between those of us who are a part of this time. The difference lies in our state of mind and motivation.

Proper motivation does not come about simply by our being aware that one kind of motivation is right and another wrong. Awareness alone does not change motivation. It takes effort. If we make this effort wisely, we will attain a positive, desirable result, but unwise effort is akin to self-torture. Therefore, we need to know how to act.

This issue of making a wise use of effort is very important. For example, even external development, such as the construction of a building, requires a tremendous amount of diligence and care. You need to take into account its exact location, the suitability of the environment, the climate and so forth. Having taken all those factors into account, you can then build a reliable and appropriate structure.

Similarly, when you make an effort in the realm of mental experience, it is important to first have a basic understanding of the nature of mind, thoughts and emotions, and also to take into account the complexity of the human physiological condition and how it interfaces with the surrounding environment.

Therefore, it is important for you to have a wide, comprehensive knowledge of things so that you don't exert all your effort blindly pursuing your goal on the basis of a single point. That's not the way of the intelligent, the way of the wise. The way of the wise is to exert effort on the basis of much wider knowledge.

In the Tibetan Buddhist tradition, there are more than one hundred volumes of *Kangyur*—sutras attributed to the Buddha himself—and more than two hundred volumes of *Tengyur*—the collection of authoritative commentaries written by such Indian masters as Nagarjuna and Asanga. If you were to distill the meaning of all of these sutras and their commentaries and incorporate them into your practice, you would make tremendous strides in terms of realization and spiritual progress, but if you treat all this great literature simply as an object of veneration and seek instead some smaller text on which to base your practice, then although you will receive some benefit, your spiritual progress will not be that great.

INTELLECTUAL AND EXPERIENTIAL UNDERSTANDING

It is important to be able to differentiate between two levels of under-standing. One is the superficial, intellectual level, where on the basis of reading, studying or listening to teachings, we distinguish between nega-tive and positive qualities of mind and recognize their nature and origin. The other is the deeper, experiential level, where we actually cultivate and generate positive qualities within ourselves.

Although it can be challenging to develop an intellectual under-standing of certain topics, it is generally easier because it can be cultivated merely by reading texts or listening to teachings. Experiential under-standing is far more difficult to develop, since it comes about only as a result of sustained practice. At the experiential level, your under-standing is also accompanied by a strong component of feeling; your understanding is essentially a felt experience.

Because experiential understanding is thus accompanied by power-ful emotions, you can see that although many emotions are destructive, there are positive emotional states as well. Actually, human beings could not survive without emotion. Emotion is an integral part of being human; without it, there would be no basis for life. However, we also know that many of our problems and conflicts are entangled with strong emotions. When certain emotions arise within our hearts and minds, they create an immediate disturbance, which isn't only temporary but can lead to negative long-term consequences, especially when we inter-act with other people. These negative emotions can also damage our physical health.

When other types of emotion arise, however, they immediately induce a sense of strength and courage, creating a more positive atmosphere in gen-eral and leading to positive long-term consequences, including our health. Putting aside the question of spiritual practice for the moment, we can see that even from the perspective of mundane day-to-day life, there are destructive emotions and those that are constructive.

The Tibetan term for Dharma is *chö*, which has the literal connotation of "changing," or "bringing about transformation." When we talk about transforming the mind, we are referring to the task of diminishing the force of destructive thoughts and emotions while developing the force of those that are constructive and beneficial. In this way, through the practice of Dharma, we transform our undisciplined mind into one that is disciplined.

THE BASIS FOR TRANSFORMATION

How do we know that it is possible to transform our mind? There are two bases for this. One is the fundamental law of impermanence; that all things and events are subject to transformation and change. If we examine this more deeply, we will realize that at every instant, everything that exists is going through a process of change. Even though, for example, we speak of yesterday's person as existing unchanged today, we are all aware at a gross, experiential level of the laws of impermanence; that, for instance, even the earth on which we live will one day come to an end.

If things and events did not have the nature of changing from moment to moment, we would be unable to explain how transformation takes place over time. When we reduce vast passages of time down to very brief ones, we can realize that things are actually changing from moment to moment. Modern technology helps us see some of these changes; the development of a biological organism, for example, can be observed through a microscope. Also, at a subtle theoretical level, certain observations indicate the extremely dynamic nature of physical reality. It is this fundamental law of nature—impermanence—that creates the potential for our own change, development and progress.

This transient and impermanent nature of reality is not to be understood in terms of something coming into being, remaining for a while and then ceasing to exist. That is not the meaning of impermanence at the subtle level. Subtle impermanence refers to the fact that the moment things and events come into existence, they are already impermanent in nature; the moment they arise, the process of their disintegration has already begun. When something comes into being from its causes and conditions, the seed of its cessation is born along with it. It is not that something comes into being and then a third factor or condition causes its disintegration. That is not how to understand impermanence. Impermanence means that as soon as something comes into being, it has already started to decay.

If you limit your understanding of impermanence to something's continuum, you will comprehend only gross impermanence. You will feel that when certain causes and conditions give rise to something, it remains unchanged as long as the factors that sustain its existence remain unchanged, and begins to disintegrate only when it encounters adverse circumstances. This is gross impermanence.

If, however, you deepen your understanding of impermanence by approaching it at the subtle level—the moment-to-moment change undergone by all phenomena—you will realize how as soon as something comes into being, its cessation has also begun.

At first you might feel that coming into being and coming to cessation are contradictory processes, but when you deepen your understanding of impermanence, you will realize that coming into being (birth) and cessation (death) are, in a sense, simultaneous. Thus, the fundamental law of impermanence (the transitory nature of all phenomena) gives us one basis for the possibility of transforming our minds.

The second premise for the possibility of transforming our minds is again one that we can perceive in the reality of the external physical world, where we see that certain things are in conflict with others. We can call this the law of contradiction. For example, heat and cold, darkness and light and so forth are opposing forces—enhancing one automatically diminishes the other. In some cases this is a gradual process, in others, instantaneous. For instance, when you switch on a light, darkness in a room is immediately dispelled.

If you look at the mental world of thoughts and emotions in the same way, you will again find many opposing forces, such that when you encourage and develop certain types of emotions, those that contradict them automatically diminish in intensity. This natural fact of our consciousness, where opposite forces contradict one another, provides another premise for the possibility of change and transformation.

When we take two types of thought or emotion that directly oppose one another, the question arises, which reflects the true state of affairs and which is a false way of relating to the world? The answer is that those thoughts and emotions that are strongly grounded in experience and reason are the ones with truth on their side, whereas those that are contrary to the way things exist, no matter how powerful they may be at any given time, are actually unstable. Since they lack valid grounding in experience and reason, they do not have a firm foundation.

Also, if we take two kinds of emotion that directly oppose one other and examine them to see what distinguishes one from the other, another feature we notice is that they differ in their long-term effects.

There are certain types of emotion that give us temporary relief or satisfaction, but when we examine them with our faculty of intelligence—the insight that enables us to judge between long- and short-term benefits and shortcomings—we find that in the long run they are destructive and harmful; they cannot be supported by reason or insight. The moment the light of intelligence shines on destructive emotions, they no longer have any support.

There are other types of emotion, however, that may seem a bit disturbing at the time but actually have long-term benefits, and are, therefore, reinforced by reason and insight, supported by intelligence.

Therefore, positive emotions are ultimately more powerful than negative ones because their potential for development is greater.

These two premises—the laws of impermanence and contradiction—allow us to see the possibility of bringing about transformation within ourselves.

INVESTIGATING THE NATURE OF REALITY

All this suggests the importance of having a deeper knowledge of the nature of the mind and its various aspects and functions in general, and the nature and complexity of emotion in particular. Also, since we realize that many of our problems arise from a fundamentally flawed way of perceiving and relating to the world, it becomes important for us to be able to examine whether or not our perception accords with the true nature of reality. Understanding the true nature of reality is crucial, as it is our perception of reality that lies at the heart of how we relate to the world. However, reality here means not just the immediate facts of our experience and environment but the entire expanse of reality, because many of our thoughts and emotions arise not only as a result of the immediate physical environment but also out of abstract ideas.

Therefore, in the Buddha's teaching, we find a great deal of discussion on the nature of reality in terms of the eighteen constituents, the twelve sources, the five aggregates and so forth[3] and how it relates to the practitioner's quest for enlightenment. If the Buddhist path were simply a matter of faith and cultivating deep devotion to the Buddha, there would have been no need for him to explain the nature of reality in such technical and complex terms. From this perspective, then, the Buddha's teaching can be described as an exploration of the nature of reality.

Just as scientific disciplines place tremendous emphasis on the need for objectivity on the part of the scientist, Buddhism also emphasizes the importance of examining the nature of reality from an objective stance.

You cannot maintain a point of view simply because you like it or because it accords with your preset metaphysical or emotional prejudices. If your view of reality is based simply on fantasy or conjecture, there will be no possibility of your being able to cultivate that view to an infinite level.

When you are engaged in the Buddhist path of the exploration of the nature of reality, there are principally two faculties at work in your mind. One is the faculty of investigation, which subjects reality to analysis. In Buddhist language this is described as "wisdom," or "insight." Then there is the faculty of "method," or "skillful means," which is the faculty that allows you to deepen your courage and tolerance and generates the powerful motivational force that sustains you in your spiritual quest.

Question. Your Holiness, you said that all phenomena are subject to impermanence. Is the pure, unobstructed nature of mind also subject to impermanence? Does this nature of mind have a birth and a death?

His Holiness. When we speak about the nature of mind in a Buddhist context, we have to understand that it can be understood on two different levels—the ultimate level of reality, where the nature of mind is understood in terms of its emptiness of inherent existence, and the relative, or conventional, level, which refers to the mere quality of luminosity, knowing and experience.

If your question relates to the mind's conventional nature, then just as the mind itself goes through a process of change and flux, so does the nature of mind. This already indicates that the nature of mind is an impermanent phenomenon. However, if you are asking about the mind's emptiness, then we need to consider that even though the mind's emptiness is not a transient phenomenon—that is, not subject to causes and conditions—it cannot be posited independent of a given object.

In other words, the emptiness of mind cannot exist independently of mind itself. The emptiness of mind is nothing other than its utter lack of intrinsic, or inherent, existence. Therefore, as different states of mind come and go, new instances of the emptiness of mind also occur.

2

FEATURES OF THE LAM-RIM TEACHINGS

Atisha's *Lamp for the Path to Enlightenment*

In terms of the lineage of the teachings of the two texts we will be following here, I first received the transmission of Lama Tsong Khapa's text, *Lines of Experience*, from Tathag Rinpoche at a very early age, and later from my most venerable tutors, the late Kyabje Ling Rinpoche, who was also the master for my full ordination as a monk, and the late Kyabje Trijang Rinpoche.

The transmission of Atisha's text, *A Lamp for the Path to Enlightenment*, was quite hard to find at one point, but I received it from my late teacher, Rigzin Tenpa, who may have received the lineage from Khangsar Dorje Chang. Later I received a teaching on it from the late Serkong Tsenshab Rinpoche, who gave the transmission in conjunction with Panchen Losang Chögyen's commentary, which he was able to present almost exclusively by heart.

Lamp for the Path: Verse 1

> Homage to the *bodhisattva*, the youthful Manjushri.
>
> I pay homage with great respect
> To the conquerors of the three times,
> To their teaching and to those who aspire to virtue.

Urged by the good disciple Jangchub Ö,
I shall illuminate the lamp
For the path to enlightenment.

The line, "Homage to the bodhisattva, the youthful Manjushri," is a salutation written by the translator who originally translated this text from Sanskrit into Tibetan. At the end of the first verse, the author states his intention for composing this text.

A Lamp for the Path to Enlightenment was composed in Tibet by the Indian master, Atisha Dipamkara Shrijnana. During the reign of the Ngari kings Lhalama Yeshe Ö and his nephew Jangchub Ö, tremendous efforts were made to invite Atisha from India to Tibet. As a result of these efforts, Lhalama Yeshe Ö was imprisoned by a neighboring anti-Buddhist king and actually lost his life, but Jangchub Ö persevered and was finally successful. When Atisha arrived in Tibet, Jangchub Ö requested him to give a teaching that would be beneficial to the entire Tibetan population. In response, therefore, Atisha wrote *A Lamp for the Path*, which makes it a unique text, because although it was written by an Indian master, it was composed in Tibet specifically for Tibetans.

THE MEANING OF THE TITLE

The title, *A Lamp for the Path to Enlightenment* has profound meaning. The Tibetan term for enlightenment is *jang-chub*, the two syllables of which refer to the two aspects of the Buddha's enlightened qualities. *Jang* connotes the enlightened quality of having overcome all obstructions, negativities and limitations. *Chub* literally means "embodiment of all knowledge" and connotes the quality of Buddha's realization and wisdom. Therefore, *jang-chub* means the Buddha's enlightened quality of having abandoned and overcome all negativities and limitations (purity) combined with the perfection of all knowledge (realization). *Jang-chub chen-po*, "great enlightenment," is an epithet for the Buddha's enlightened state. The title, *A Lamp for the Path to Enlightenment*, suggests that this text presents the method, or process, by which we can actualize this state of enlightenment.

When we speak about enlightenment and the path leading to it, we are naturally speaking about a quality, or state, of mind. In the final analysis, enlightenment is nothing other than a perfected state of mind. Enlightenment should not be understood as some kind of physical location or rank or status that is conferred upon us. It is the state of mind where all negativities and limitations have been purified, and all potentials of positive qualities fully perfected and realized.

Since the ultimate objective is a state of mind, the methods and paths by which it is attained must also be states of mind. Enlightenment cannot be attained by external means, only through an internal process. As we develop and improve our states of mind, our knowledge, wisdom and realization gradually increase, culminating in our attainment of enlightenment.

The metaphor of the lamp is used because just as a lamp dispels darkness, the teachings in this text dispel the darkness of misunderstanding with respect to the path to enlightenment. Just as a lamp illuminates whatever objects lie in its sphere, this text shines a light on all the various elements and subtle points of the path leading to full enlightenment.

THE OBJECTS OF SALUTATION

The objects of salutation in this verse—the "conquerors of the three times"—are the Three Jewels of Refuge. It is important to pay homage to the Buddha not as just some noble object but in terms of the meaning of *jang-chub*. The Sanskrit term for *jang-chub* is *bodhi*, which conveys a sense of awakening—a state where all knowledge and realization have been perfected. Therefore, when explaining the meaning of awakening, or enlightenment, we can speak about both the process by which this awakening takes place and the state to which awakening brings us; in other words, the means and the fruition.

When we understand enlightenment as a resultant state, we are primarily referring to the enlightened quality of purity—the perfected state where all negativities and limitations have been purified. There is another aspect to this purity, which is the primordially pure nature of the enlightened state. The reason why enlightenment is a perfected state where all obscurations have been purified is because natural purity is its fundamental basis.

When we understand enlightenment as a process, or instrument, by which awakening is experienced, we are referring to the Buddha's enlightened quality of wisdom. This is the *dharmakaya*, the buddha-body of reality, the "wisdom body," or "wisdom embodiment," of the Buddha, and it is this wisdom that brings about the perfection and purification.

Thus we can understand the significance of the explanations of the different types of *nirvana* in the scriptures. For example, we speak of "natural nirvana," "nirvana with residue," "nirvana without residue," and "non-abiding nirvana." Natural nirvana refers to the fundamentally pure nature of reality, where all things and events are devoid of any inherent, intrinsic or independent reality. This is the fundamental ground. It is our misconception of this fundamental reality that gives rise to all the delusions and their derivative thoughts and emotions.

No matter how powerful the false perceptions of reality may be at any given time, if we subject them to scrutiny we will find that they have no grounding in reason or experience. On the other hand, the more we cultivate the correct understanding of emptiness as the nature of reality (and relate this understanding to actual reality), the more we will be able to affirm and develop it, because it is a correct way of perceiving the world. Flawed perceptions lack grounding, experience and reasoning, whereas grounding, experience and reasoning support the understanding of emptiness. Thus we will come to understand that this highest antidote—the wisdom of emptiness—can be developed and enhanced to its fullest potential. This is the understanding of natural nirvana, which makes possible the attainment of the other nirvanas.

What is this natural nirvana that serves as the basis for attaining such purity and perfection? On what grounds do we know that such an ultimate nature of reality exists? We can answer these questions from everyday experience. We are all aware of the fundamental fact that there is often a gap between the way we perceive things and the way things really are. This disparity between our perception of reality and the actual state of affairs leads to all kinds of problems and confusion. However, we also know that our perception sometimes *does* correspond to reality accurately.

If we go further, we will see that there are two levels of reality. At one level—that of conventional, or relative, reality—worldly conventions operate and our perception and understanding of things and events is based purely upon the way that things appear to us. However, when we question the ultimate status of things and events and the way that they really exist, we enter another realm, or level—that of ultimate reality.

THE TWO TRUTHS

Buddhism discusses what are known as the two truths—the truths of conventional and ultimate reality. The concept of two levels of reality is not unique to Buddhism. It is a common epistemological approach in many of the ancient Indian schools. Followers of the non-Buddhist Samkhya school, for example, explain reality in terms of twenty-five categories of phenomena.[4] The self [Skt: *purusha* Tib: *kye-bu*] and the primal substance [Skt: *prakriti*; Tib: *rang-zhin*] are said to be ultimate truths, while the remaining twenty-three categories of phenomena are said to be manifestations, or expressions, of this underlying reality. However, what is unique in Mahayana, particularly in the Madhyamaka, or Middle Way, School, is that conventional and ultimate truths are not seen as two unrelated, independent entities but as different perspectives of one and the same world.

According to the Middle Way School of Buddhism, the ultimate truth, or the ultimate nature of reality, is the emptiness of all things and events. In trying to understand the meaning of this emptiness, we can turn to the teachings of the Indian master, Nagarjuna, who brought together all the various understandings of emptiness into the single statement that emptiness must be understood in terms of dependent origination.

When we talk about emptiness, what we are negating or denying is the possibility of things or events having inherent existence. This suggests that all things and events come into being purely as a result of the gathering of causes and conditions, regardless of how complex the nexus of these causes and conditions may be. It is within this nexus of causes and conditions that we can understand the complexity and multiplicity of the world of experience.

There is great diversity in the everyday world of experience, including our own immediately relevant experiences of pain and pleasure. Even pain and pleasure are not independently existent real experiences; they also come into being as a result of causes or conditions. No thing or event possesses the reality of independence and is, therefore, thoroughly contingent, or dependent. The very existence of all phenomena depends upon other factors. It is this absence of independent status that is the meaning behind terms such as "emptiness" and "the emptiness of inherent existence."

The Four Noble Truths

If we examine the nature of reality more deeply, we will find that within this complex world, there are things and events that have a certain degree of permanence, at least from the point of view of their continuum. Examples of this include the continuity of consciousness and the mind's essential nature of luminosity and clarity. There is nothing that can threaten the continuity of consciousness or the essential nature of mind. Then there are certain types of experiences and events in the world that appear evident at a particular point but cease to exist after contact with opposing forces; such phenomena can be understood to be adventitious, or circumstantial. It is on the basis of these two categories of phenomena that the teachings of the Four Noble Truths, such as the truths of suffering and its origin, become relevant.

When we further examine this dynamic, complex and diverse world that we experience, we find that phenomena can also be categorized in three ways:

1. The world of matter.
2. The world of consciousness, or subjective experience.
3. The world of abstract entities.

First, there is the world of physical reality, which we can experience through our senses; that is, tangible objects that have material properties.

Second, there is the category of phenomena that are purely of the nature of subjective experience, such as our perception of the world. As I mentioned earlier, we are often confronted by a gap between the way we perceive things and the way they really are. Sometimes we know that there is a correspondence; sometimes we know there is a disparity. This points towards a subjective quality that all sentient beings possess. This is the world of experience, such as the feeling dimension of pain and pleasure.

Third, there are phenomena that are abstract in nature, such as our concept of time, including past, present and future, and even our concepts of years, months and days. These and other abstract ideas can be understood only in relation to some concrete reality such as physical entities.

Although they do not enjoy a reality of their own, we still experience and participate in them.[5] In Buddhist texts, then, the taxonomy of reality is often presented under these three broad categories.

Out of this complex world of reality that we experience and participate in, how do the Four Noble Truths directly relate to our experiences of pain and pleasure? The basic premise of the Four Noble Truths is recognition of the very fundamental nature we all share—the natural and instinctual desire to attain happiness and overcome suffering. When we refer to suffering here, we do not mean only immediate experiences such as painful sensations. From the Buddhist point of view, even the very physical and mental bases from which these painful experiences arise—the five aggregates [Skt: *skandha*] of form, feeling, discriminative awareness, conditioning factors and consciousness—are suffering in nature. At a fundamental level, the underlying conditioning that we all share is also recognized as *dukkha*, or suffering.

What gives rise to these sufferings? What are the causes and conditions that create them? Of the Four Noble Truths, the first two truths—suffering and its origin—relate to the causal process of the suffering that we all naturally wish to avoid. It is only by ensuring that the causes and conditions of suffering are not created or, if the cause has been created, that the conditions do not become complete, that we can prevent the consequences from ripening. One of the fundamental aspects of the law of causality is that if all the causes and conditions are fully gathered, there is no force in the universe that can prevent their fruition. This is how we can understand the dynamic between suffering and its origin.

The last two truths—cessation of suffering and the path to its cessation—relate to the experience of happiness to which we all naturally aspire. Cessation—the total pacification of suffering and its causes—refers to the highest form of happiness, which is neither a feeling nor an experience; the path—the methods and processes by which cessation is

FEATURES OF THE LAM-RIM TEACHINGS

attained—is its cause. Therefore, the last two truths relate to the causal process of happiness.

THE THREE JEWELS: BUDDHA, DHARMA AND SANGHA

There are two principal origins of suffering—karma and the emotional and mental afflictions that underlie and motivate karmic actions. Karma is rooted in and motivated by mental defilements, or afflictions, which are the primary roots of our suffering and cyclic existence. Therefore, it is important for practitioners to cultivate three understandings:

1. The fundamental nature of consciousness is luminous and pure.
2. Afflictions can be purified—separated from the essential nature of mind.
3. There are powerful antidotes that can be applied to counter the defilements and afflictions.

You should develop the recognition of the possibility of a true cessation of suffering on the basis of these three facts. True cessation is what is meant by the Jewel of Dharma, the second of the Three Jewels. Dharma also refers to the path to the cessation of suffering—the direct realization of emptiness. Once you have this deeper understanding of the meaning of Dharma as true cessation of suffering and the wisdom that brings it about, you will also recognize that there are different levels of cessation. The first level of cessation is attained on the path of seeing, when you directly realize emptiness and become an *arya*. As you gradually progress through the further levels of purification, you gain higher and higher levels of cessation.

Once you have understood Dharma in terms of both cessation and the path, you can recognize the possibility of Sangha, the practitioners who embody these qualities. And once you have understood

the possibility of Sangha, you can also envision the possibility of someone who has perfected all the qualities of Dharma. Such a person is a
Buddha—a fully enlightened being.

In this way, you will be able to gain a deeper understanding of the
meaning of the Three Jewels: the Jewel of Buddha, the Jewel of Dharma
and the Jewel of Sangha. Furthermore, you will recognize the possibility of attaining this state of perfection yourself, and a deep yearning or
aspiration to do so will arise in you. Thus, you will be able to cultivate
faith in the Three Jewels; faith that is not simply admiration, but something that arises from a deep understanding of the teachings of the Four
Noble Truths and the two truths and enables you to emulate the states
of the Buddha, Dharma and Sangha.

In terms of an individual practitioner's sequence of realization, first and
foremost is the Jewel of Dharma. When you actualize Dharma within yourself, you become Sangha—an arya being. As you develop your realization of
Dharma, you reach higher and higher levels of the path, culminating in the
attainment of the full enlightenment or Buddhahood. Dharma is the true
refuge, Sangha comes next, and finally Buddha.

In the historical context, Buddha came first because Shakyamuni
Buddha came into being as an emanation body [Skt: *nirmanakaya*]
and then turned the wheel of Dharma by giving the scriptural teachings.
By practicing the Buddha's teachings, some of his disciples realized the
Dharma and became Sangha. Although historically Dharma comes
second, in terms of an individual's sequence of realization, it comes
first.

Lama Tsong Khapa's *Lines of Experience*

This text, which is also known as the *Abbreviated Points of the Stages of
the Path to Enlightenment*, is the shortest of Lama Tsong Khapa's lam-rim
commentaries expounding the teachings of Atisha's *Lamp*.

The style and structure of the genre of teachings known as lam-rim, which can be translated as "stages of the path" or "graded course to enlightenment," follow the arrangement of Atisha's *Lamp*, and the way they are set up allows any individual, regardless of his or her level of realization, to put into practice the appropriate teachings. All the steps of the meditation practices are arranged in a logical, sequential way, so that the practitioner can traverse the path step by step, knowing what to practice now and what to practice next.

The reason that this text is sometimes called *Songs of Experience* is because Lama Tsong Khapa has distilled all his experience and understanding of the lam-rim teachings into these verses and expressed them in the style of a spontaneous song of spiritual realization.

The term *lam-rim* has great significance and suggests the importance of the following three points:

1. The practitioner has correct recognition and understanding of the nature of the path in which he or she is engaged.
2. All the key elements of the path and practices are complete.
3. The practitioner engages in all the elements of the practices in the correct sequence.

With respect to the first point, the need for correct understanding of the nature of the path, let us take the example of *bodhicitta*, the altruistic intention. If you understand the altruistic intention to mean solely the *aspiration* to bring about the welfare of other sentient beings, your understanding of this particular aspect of the path is incomplete and inadequate. True bodhicitta is a non-simulated, spontaneous and natural *experience* of this altruistic intention. This is how you may mistake a mere intellectual understanding of bodhicitta for a true realization. It is, therefore, very important to be able to identify the nature of specific aspects of the path.

The second point, that all the key elements of the path should be complete, is also critical. As I mentioned before, much of the suffering we experience arises from our complex psychological afflictions. These emotional and mental afflictions are so diverse that we need a wide diversity of antidotes. Although it is theoretically possible for a single antidote to counteract all our afflictions, in reality it is very difficult to find such a panacea. Therefore, we need to cultivate a number of specific antidotes that relate to specific types of afflictions. If, for example, people are building a very complex structure such as a spacecraft, they need to assemble an enormous variety of machines and other equipment. In the mental and experiential world, we need an even greater diversity of means.

With respect to afflictions of the mind and flawed ways of perceiving and relating to the world, Buddhist texts speak of four principal false views:

1. The false view of perceiving impermanent phenomena as permanent.
2. The false view of perceiving events, our own existence and the various aggregates as desirable when they are not.
3. The false view of perceiving suffering experiences as happiness.
4. The false view of perceiving our own existence and the world as self-existent and independent when they are utterly devoid of self-existence and independence.

In order to counteract these false views, we need to cultivate all the various elements of the path. This is why there is a need for completeness.

The third point is that we're not just accumulating material things and collecting them in a room; we're trying to transform our mind. The stages of this transformation must evolve in the right order. First, we subdue gross negative emotions, then the subtle ones.

There is a natural sequence to Dharma practice. When we cultivate a path such as bodhicitta, gross levels of understanding, such as the simulated, deliberately cultivated ones, arise sooner than spontaneous, genuine experiences and realizations. Similarly, we need to cultivate the practices for attaining higher rebirths and other favorable conditions of existence before cultivating those for attaining enlightenment.

These three points—correct understanding of the nature of the path, its completeness and practicing its various elements in the right sequence—are all suggested in the term "lam-rim."

THE ORIGIN OF THE LAM-RIM TEACHINGS: THE GREATNESS OF THE AUTHORS

A great number of commentaries came into being on the basis of Atisha's root text, *A Lamp for the Path to Enlightenment*. Among these is the genre of writings by the Kadampa masters known as *ten-rim*, or *Presentation of the Stages of the Path*, as well as Lama Tsong Khapa's lam-rim works. These teachings present different skillful means for teaching the Dharma, but they are all grounded in the writings of authentic Indian masters. In the texts of some of the early Indian masters, we find what is known as "the five methods of teaching" or "the five aspects of the skillful means of teaching."

Later, at Nalanda Monastic University,[6] a unique tradition of presenting the Dharma to students developed— the skillful means of "the three purifications" or "the three pure factors":

1. Ensuring that the teaching being given is pure.
2. Ensuring that the teacher giving the teaching is pure.
3. Ensuring that the students receiving the teaching are pure.

With respect to the second pure factor, even though the teaching being given may be pure, if the teacher giving it lacks the necessary qualities and qualifications, there will be shortcomings in the presentation. It thus became a tradition that before teaching the Dharma, teachers had to receive permission to do so from their own masters. With respect to the third pure factor, even though the teaching and the teacher may be pure, if the students' minds are not properly prepared, then even an authentic teaching may not bestow much benefit. Therefore, the third pure factor means to ensure that the motivation of the listeners is pure.

Later on, when the Buddhadharma underwent a period of decline in the Nalanda area, it began to flourish in Bengal, particularly at Vikramashila Monastery, where a new tradition in the style of teaching emerged. Here it became customary to begin a teaching by talking about the greatness of the person who composed the text, the greatness and quality of the teaching itself, and the procedure by which the teaching and the listening of that teaching would take place, before moving on to the fourth skillful means, teaching the actual procedure for guiding the disciple along the path to enlightenment.

In those days, the majority of the people sustaining and developing the Dharma in the land of the noble beings, ancient India, were monastics, most notably monks from monasteries like Nalanda and Vikramashila. If you look at the masters from these great centers of learning, you will understand how they upheld the Buddhadharma. They were not only practitioners of the Bodhisattvayana, having taken bodhisattva vows, but also practitioners of the Vajrayana. Nevertheless, the daily life of all these practitioners was very much grounded in the teachings of the *vinaya*—the teachings on monastic ethics. The vinaya teachings of the Buddha were the actual foundation upon which these monasteries were established and maintained. Two stories illustrate how seriously these great institutions took their monastic discipline.

The great Yogachara thinker and highly realized master

Dharmapala, who became the main source of the great inspirational teachings of the Sakya *lam-dre*—path and fruition—teachings, was a monk at Nalanda Monastery. In addition to being a monk, he was also a great practitioner of Vajrayana and later became known as the mahasiddha Virupa. One day, while the disciplinarian of the monastery was on his rounds, he looked into Dharmapala's room and saw that it was full of women. In fact, this great mystic tantric master was emanating *dakinis*, but since monks were not allowed to have women in their room, Dharmapala was expelled from the monastery. It didn't matter that his infraction was a display of high levels of tantric realization; the fact remained that Dharmapala had broken the codes of monastic discipline and had to go.

There is a similar story about the great Indian master Nagarjuna, founder of the Middle Way School, whom all Mahayana Buddhists revere. At one time, the entire Nalanda area was experiencing a terrible drought and everybody was starving. Through alchemy, Nagarjuna is said to have transformed base metals into gold to help alleviate the famine, which had also affected the monastery. However, the practice of alchemy was a breach of the monastic code and Nagarjuna, too, was expelled from the monastery.

Lines of Experience: Verse 1

> I prostrate before you, (Buddha), head of the Shakya clan.
> Your enlightened body is born out of tens of millions of
> positive virtues and perfect accomplishments; your
> enlightened speech grants the wishes of limitless beings;
> your enlightened mind sees all knowables as they are.

As we have seen, it is traditional first to present the greatness of the author in order to explain the validity and authenticity of the teaching and its lineage. Therefore, the first verse of Lama Tsong Khapa's *Lines of Experience* is a salutation to the Buddha. There is a Tibetan saying that just as a pure stream of water must have its source in pure mountain snow, an authentic teaching of the Dharma must have its origin in the teachings of Shakyamuni Buddha. That is why there is such emphasis placed on the lineage of the teachings.

In this verse, then, the author reflects upon the qualities of the Buddha's body, speech and mind. The qualities of Buddha's body are presented from the point of view of the perfection of the causes that have created it. The qualities of the Buddha's speech are presented from the point of view of the perfect fruits of his speech, the fulfillment of the wishes of all sentient beings. The qualities of the Buddha's enlightened mind are presented from the point of view of its nature and attributes.

In this way, Lama Tsong Khapa pays homage to Shakyamuni Buddha, who was born into the Shakya family and is chief among all humans. When he writes, "I prostrate before you," he is saying "I bow and touch my head to the lowest part of your body."

One of the reasons for stating the causes and qualities of the Buddha's body is to suggest that the Buddha's enlightened body has not existed since beginningless time. It was not there right from the start but has been created and acquired. The Buddha's enlightened body did not come into being without cause; it was attained through causes and conditions that are compatible with the actual enlightened state. A detailed explanation of the causal relationship between the various practices and the Buddha's enlightened embodiments can be found in Nagarjuna's *Precious Garland (Ratnavali).*[7]

The second sentence describes the quality of the Buddha's enlightened speech as fulfilling the wishes of limitless sentient beings. This explains the actual purpose of attaining enlightenment, which is to benefit other sentient beings. When we become fully enlightened, it is our duty to serve all sentient beings and fulfill their wishes. There are countless ways in which enlightened beings serve sentient beings, such as using their enlightened minds to discern the tremendous diversity of sentient beings' needs and to display miraculous powers, but the primary medium used by fully enlightened beings to fulfill the wishes of sentient beings is their enlightened speech. The term "limitless beings" suggests that the Buddha uses his enlightened speech in limitless skillful ways.

We also find this respect for the diversity of practitioners' mental dispositions in the teachings of Shakyamuni Buddha. For example, in acknowledgement of the multiplicity of practitioners' motives, courage and ethical commitment, we find the three vehicles: the Hearer Vehicle (Shravakayana), the Solitary Buddha Vehicle (Pratyekabuddhayana) and the Bodhisattva Vehicle (Mahayana). Then, from the point of view of the wide range of philosophical inclinations, we find the Buddha's teachings on the four main schools: Vaibhashika, Sautrantika, Cittamatra (Mind Only) and Madhyamaka, or Middle Way.

According to the Mahayana scriptures, we can understand the teachings of the Buddha in terms of what are known as the "three turnings of the wheel of Dharma."[8] The first turning of the wheel was at Sarnath, near Varanasi, and was the first public sermon that the Buddha gave. The main subject of this teaching was the Four Noble Truths, in which the Buddha laid the basic framework of the entire Buddhadharma and the path to enlightenment.

The second turning of the wheel of Dharma was at Vulture Peak, near Rajgir, in present-day Bihar. The main teachings presented here were those on the perfection of wisdom. In these sutras, the Buddha elaborated on the third Noble Truth, the truth of cessation. The perfection of wisdom teachings are critical to fully understanding the Buddha's teaching on the truth of cessation, particularly to fully recognizing the basic purity of mind and the possibility of cleansing it of all pollutants. The explicit subject matter of the *Perfection of Wisdom Sutras (Prajnaparamita)* is the doctrine of emptiness. Then, as the basis for the emptiness teachings, these sutras present the entire path in what is known as the hidden, or concealed, subject matter of the *Perfection of Wisdom Sutras*, which is elaborated in a very clear and systematic way in Maitreya's *Ornament of Clear Realization (Abhisamayalamkara)*.

The third turning of the wheel is a collection of sutras taught in different times and places. The principal sutras in this category of teachings are the source material for Maitreya's *Uttaratantra*. Not only do they present emptiness as taught in the second turning of the wheel but they also present the quality of the subjective experience. Although these sutras do not talk about the subjective experience in terms of the subtleties of levels, they do present the subjective quality of wisdom and the levels through which one can enhance it and are known as the *Tathagatagarbha (Essence, or Nucleus, of Buddhahood) Sutras*. Among Nagarjuna's writings there is a collection of hymns along with a collection of what could be called an analytic corpus, such as his *Fundamentals of the Middle Way*. The analytic corpus deals directly with the teachings on emptiness as taught in the *Perfection of Wisdom Sutras*, whereas the hymns relate more to the *Tathagatagarbha Sutras*.

The last line in this verse, "Your enlightened mind sees all knowables as they are," presents the quality of the Buddha's enlightened mind. The reference to "all knowables" refers to the entire expanse of reality, which encompasses both conventional and ultimate levels. The ability to directly realize both levels of reality within a single instant of thought is said to be the mark of an enlightened mind. This ability is a consequence of the individual having overcome and cleansed not only the afflictions of thought and emotion but also the subtle traces and propensities of these afflictions.

Lines of Experience: Verse 2

I prostrate before you Maitreya and Manjushri,

> supreme spiritual children of this peerless teacher.
> Assuming responsibility (to further) all Buddha's
> enlightened deeds, you sport emanations to countless
> worlds.

In this verse, the author makes salutations to Maitreya and Manjushri and states that they are the two principal disciples of Shakyamuni Buddha. According to the Mahayana scriptures, when the Buddha taught the Mahayana sutras, Maitreya and Manjushri were the principal disciples present. In the Mahayana tradition, we list eight main bodhisattva disciples of Shakyamuni Buddha.[9] However, we should not understand these bodhisattvas as having a physical presence at the Buddha's teachings but rather as being present on a subtler level of reality. The significance of singling out Maitreya and Manjushri is that Maitreya is regarded as the custodian and medium of the Buddha's teachings on skillful means and Manjushri is regarded as the custodian and medium of the Buddha's teachings on the profound view of emptiness.

Lines of Experience: Verse 3

> I prostrate before your feet, Nagarjuna and Asanga,
> ornaments of our Southern Continent. Highly famed
> throughout the three realms,[10] you have commented on
> the most difficult to fathom "Mother of the Buddhas"
> (*Perfection of Wisdom Sutras*) according to exactly what
> was intended.

In this verse, the author makes salutations to Nagarjuna and Asanga, who became the custodians and progenitors of the two aspects of the Buddha's teaching: Asanga was the progenitor of the path of skillful means and Nagarjuna was the progenitor of the path of the profound view of emptiness. Lama Tsong Khapa pays homage to these Indian masters as great revitalizers of the Buddha's teachings. Historically, Nagarjuna came to earth around four hundred years after the death of the Buddha, and Asanga about two hundred years after the death of Nagarjuna. In light of this distance of time between them, the question immediately arises as to the continuum, or lineage, between the Buddha and Nagarjuna and Asanga.

We can understand the continuity of the teachings through successive living masters in human form, such as the lineage of the transmission of the vinaya teachings of ethical discipline, but the transmission of the lineage can also be understood on a more subtle level. For example, the celestial form of the bodhisattva Manjushri had a special connection with Nagarjuna, and Maitreya had a special connection with Asanga. Thus, the great bodhisattvas may sometimes directly inspire the lineage.

When we look at the transmission of the Buddha's teachings in this way, it obviously raises questions about the status of the historical Buddha. In the Buddhist tradition, there are generally two perspectives on this. One views Shakyamuni Buddha in conventional terms. At the initial stage, he is seen as an ordinary being who, through meditation and practice, attained enlightenment in that very lifetime under the bodhi tree. From this point of view, the instant before his enlightenment, the Buddha was an unenlightened being.

The other perspective, which is presented in Maitreya's *Uttaratantra*, considers the twelve major deeds of the Buddha as actions of a fully enlightened being and the historical Buddha is seen as an emanation body. This nirmanakaya, or buddha-body of perfect emanation, must have its source in the subtler level of embodiment that is called the *sambhogakaya*, the buddha-body of perfect resource. These form bodies (*rupakaya*) are embodiments of the Buddha that arise from an ultimate level of reality, or dharmakaya. For this wisdom body to arise, however, there must be an underlying reality, which is the natural purity that I referred to before. Therefore, we also speak about the natural buddha-body (svabhavikakaya). In the Mahayana teachings, we understand Buddhahood in terms of the embodiment of these four kayas, or enlightened bodies of the Buddha.

Maitreya makes the point that while immutably abiding in the expanse of dharmakaya, the Buddha assumes diverse manifestations. Therefore, all the subsequent deeds of the Buddha, such as becoming conceived in his mother's womb, taking birth and so forth are each said to be deeds of an enlightened being. It is in this way that we can understand the connection between the lineage masters of the Mahayana sutras.

Due to the complexity of this evolution, questions have been raised as to the authenticity of the Mahayana sutras. In fact, similar questions arose even in Nagarjuna's time. In his *Precious Garland,* there is a section where he presents various arguments for the validity of the Mahayana scriptures as authentic sutras of the Buddha.[11] Similarly, in Maitreya's *Ornament of the Mahayana Sutras (Mahayanasutralamkara),* there is a section that validates the Mahayana scriptures as authentic sutras. Subsequent Mahayana masters have also written validations of the Mahayana scriptures.

One of the grounds upon which the authenticity of the Mahayana sutras has been disputed is the historical fact that when the Buddha's scriptural discourses were originally collected and compiled, they did not include any Mahayana sutras. This suggests that Mahayana scriptures such as the *Perfection of Wisdom Sutras* were not taught by the Buddha in a conventional public context but were taught to a select group of practitioners at a higher and purer level of reality. Furthermore, although there are a few cases where the Buddha taught tantra while retaining his appearance as a fully ordained monk, he taught many of the tantras by assuming the identity of the principal deity of the mandala, such as Guhyasamaja when teaching the *Guhyasamaja Tantra.* There is no reason, therefore, why these tantras had to have been taught during the time of the historical Buddha.

To understand many of these issues from a Mahayana point of view, it is important to understand Buddhahood in terms of the embodiment of the four kayas. Lama Tsong Khapa, for example, was born three hundred years after the death of the great Atisha. Once when Lama Tsong Khapa was at Retreng, the monastery of Atisha's most famous disciple, Dromtönpa, he engaged in the deep study and practice of Atisha's *Lamp for the Path*. According to his biography, during this period he had vivid encounters with Atisha and Atisha's two principal disciples, as if face-to-face. This didn't happen just once or twice but several times over a period of months. During this time, Lama Tsong Khapa spontaneously wrote the verses for the lineage masters of the lam-rim teachings.

It is said that it is possible for individuals who are karmically ready and receptive to have encounters with great beings because, even though their physical bodies may have disappeared, their wisdom embodiment remains. Even in our own lifetime there have been practitioners who have had deep, mystical encounters with masters of the past. Only by understanding the nature of buddhahood in terms of the four kayas can we make sense of these complex issues.

Lines of Experience: Verse 4

> I bow to Dipamkara (Atisha), holder of a treasure of instructions (as seen in your *Lamp for the Path to Enlightenment*). All the complete, unmistaken points concerning the paths of profound view and vast action, transmitted intact from these two great forerunners, can be included within it.

In this verse, Lama Tsong Khapa makes salutations to Atisha Dipamkara Shrijnana. Atisha was an Indian master from Bengal, which is near present-day Dhaka in Bangladesh. He had many teachers, but the principal among them was Serlingpa, who came from the island of Serling, the "Land of Gold." Although there seems to be a place with the same name in the southern part of Thailand, according to Tibetan sources it took eighteen months for Atisha to reach the island by boat from India, which suggests that it was much further away than Thailand. There seems to be a great deal more evidence for Serling having been located somewhere in Indonesia, probably around Java, and, in fact, some reference to the master Serlingpa that has been found in that area.[12]

Atisha received the instructions on the practice bodhicitta from this master. He then received many teachings on the profound view of emptiness from another master, Rigpa'i Khuchug (Vidyakokila the younger, or Avadhutipa). The general understanding is that until Atisha's time, wisdom and method (or emptiness and skillful means) were transmitted as two distinct lineages, even though the masters practiced them in union. It was Atisha who unified the two, and the profound view and vast practice were transmitted together from then on.[13]

From Atisha's principal student and the custodian of his teachings, Dromtönpa, there evolved three main lineages of the Kadam order.[14] The first was the Kadam Shungpawa, the "Kadampa Treatise Followers," which was handed down through Dromtönpa's disciple, Potowa, and emphasized study of the major Indian treatises. The second was the Kadam Lamrimpa, the "Kadampa Lam-rim Followers," where emphasis was placed on a gradual approach to the path to enlightenment, relying more on middling versions of the treatises rather than the great ones. Then, a third lineage evolved, the Kadam Mengagpa, the "Kadampa Instruction Followers," which relied more on actual instruction from the teacher and emphasized the immediate practice of visualization and analytical meditation.

Potowa's principal student was Sharawa, a very famous master highly respected for his learning of the great treatises. One of Sharawa's contemporaries was Patsab Lotsawa, the great translator of Chandrakirti's texts from Sanskrit into Tibetan. It seems that before Patsab Lotsawa's time, Chandrakirti's works were not available in the Tibetan language. In fact, when Atisha taught Madhyamaka in Tibet, he used mainly Bhavaviveka's texts, such as the *Heart of the Middle Way (Madhyamakahridaya)* and *Blaze of Reasoning (Tarkajvala)*. During Sharawa's time, however, Patsab Lotsawa began his translation of Chandrakirti's *Supplement to the Middle Way (Madhyamakavatara)*.

It is said that when Patsab Lotsawa finished the first draft, he presented the manuscript to Sharawa and asked for his opinion. Although Sharawa did not understand Sanskrit, he made critical annotations in key areas of the text and put forward a number of suggestions and corrections. Later, when Patsab Lotsawa compared Sharawa's comments to the original Sanskrit that he had used for the translation, he discovered that Sharawa had noted the exact areas that needed revision. Patsab Lotsawa was so impressed that he praised Sharawa's tremendous depth of knowledge of Middle Way philosophy.

Later, after Sharawa received the revised copy of the *Madhyamakavatara*, he often publicly acknowledged the great contribution made by Patsab Lotsawa in bringing this new literature to Tibet. At one of Sharawa's teaching sessions, a devotee made an offering of a small piece of brown sugar to each member of the audience. It is said that Sharawa picked up a handful, threw it up into the air and said, "May this offering be to the great Patsab, who made the tremendous contribution of bringing Chandrakirti's works to the Tibetan people."

It seems that the Tibetan translators working from Sanskrit sources were tremendously learned and courageous individuals. They were also extremely faithful to the original texts. So much so that even today, modern scholars praise the accuracy of the Tibetan translations. Even though the population of Tibet is fairly small, the teachings of the Buddha have flourished there for almost 1,500 years, and over this time, many highly learned Tibetan masters have composed spiritual texts; not just monks, but lay practitioners as well.

There is a commentary on the *Hundred Thousand Verses of the Perfection of Wisdom* in the *Tengyur,* the canon containing all the translated Indian treatises. When Lama Tsong Khapa scrutinized this text, he found so many Tibetan expressions and peculiarly Tibetan ways of saying things, that he concluded that it was not an Indian treatise but an original Tibetan work. He then found corroboration of his conclusion in a catalogue, which listed this text as having been composed by the eighth century Tibetan monarch, Trisong Detsen.

In the salutation in Verse 4, Lama Tsong Khapa refers to Atisha as a "holder of a treasure of instructions." This is a reference to Atisha's *Lamp for the Path to Enlightenment.* Although the *Lamp* is quite a short text, it is extremely comprehensive in its subject matter and contains very profound instructions. According to traditional explanations, it is regarded as the instructions of Maitreya's *Ornament of Clear Realization* in distilled form.

The main source for Atisha's *Lamp* is a section in the second chapter of Maitreya's text. In stating the sequence of the path and practices, Maitreya talks about cultivating faith in the Three Jewels and the altruistic intention. He goes on to describe taking the bodhicitta vow and engaging in the path by embodying the ideals of the bodhisattva through the practice of the six perfections,[15] and then explains how to engage in the cultivation of wisdom where there is a union between calm abiding *(shamatha)* and penetrative insight *(vipashyana).* This is how the Tibetan tradition understands the source of inspiration for Atisha's text.

Lines of Experience: Verse 5

> Respectfully, I prostrate before my spiritual masters.
> You are the eyes allowing us to behold all the infinite

scriptural pronouncements, the best ford for those of
good fortune to cross to liberation. You make everything clear through your skillful deeds, which are
moved by intense loving concern.

In this verse, Lama Tsong Khapa makes salutations to the lineage masters responsible for maintaining and transmitting the practices of the
lam-rim teachings. There is a saying attributed to one of the Kadampa
masters: "Whenever I teach lam-rim, the great scriptures shudder and
say, 'This old monk is extracting our heart.'"

Lama Tsong Khapa died about six hundred years ago. Of his three
main lam-rim texts, the *Great Exposition of the Stages of the Path* is the
most important, but in all three, he presents the elements of the path to
enlightenment—the profound view of emptiness and the vast practice
of skillful means—in varying degrees of detail, introducing the essential
points of these practices in a systematic way such that even today, we can
study, contemplate and implement them in our meditation practice.

Regardless of whether the term "lam-rim" or "stages of the path" is
used, all traditions of Tibetan Buddhism—the old translation school,
the Nyingma, and the new translation schools, such as the Sakya and
Kagyü—have equivalent teachings that emphasize the foundational
practices. Furthermore, the teachings of all four schools of Tibetan
Buddhism can be validated by tracing their origins back to the writings
of authentic Indian masters.

In the tradition of the Nyingma School of Tibetan Buddhism, for
example, there is the genre of teachings known as *terma*, or "texts of rev-
elation," and another known as *kama*, or "scriptural teachings."
However, even teachings of the revealed tradition must be grounded in
those of the scriptural category. In fact, the Nyingma tradition states
that the teachings of the revealed texts should be regarded as more for
simply channeling one's focus and sharpening one's practice.

THE GREATNESS OF THE LAM-RIM TEACHINGS

Lines of Experience: Verses 6 & 7

The stages of the path to enlightenment have been transmitted intact by those who have followed in order both from Nagarjuna and Asanga, those crowning jewels of all erudite masters of our Southern Continent and the banner of whose fame stands out above the masses. As (following these stages) can fulfill every desirable aim of all nine kinds of being,[16] they are a power-granting king of precious instruction. Because they collect the streams of thousands of excellent classics, they are indeed an ocean of illustrious, correct explanation.

These teachings make it easy to understand how there is nothing contradictory in all the Buddha's teachings and make every scriptural pronouncement without exception dawn on your mind as a personal instruction. They make it easy to discover what the Buddha intended and protect you as well from the abyss of the great error. Because of these (four benefits), what discriminating person among the erudite masters of India and Tibet would not have his or her mind be completely enraptured by these stages of the path (arranged) according to the three levels of motivation, the supreme instruction to which many fortunate ones have devoted themselves?

These two verses present the greatness and quality of the lam-rim teachings.

Verse 6 explains the nature and lineage of the teaching, while Verse 7 explains its benefits.

1. *There is nothing contradictory.* One of the greatnesses of the lam-rim tradition is that these teachings enable you to recognize that there are no contradictions in any of the teachings of the Buddha. If you look at the diversity of teachings in the Mahayana scriptures, you will find that certain practices are sometimes prohibited while at other times they are encouraged. If you understand the significance of this diversity, however, you will understand that these teachings are contingent upon the different levels or capacities of the practitioners to whom they have been given. Atisha organized the entire teaching of the Buddha into the three "capacities," or "scopes," according to the abilities of different practitioners. Therefore, practices that are restricted for some are encouraged for others. If you don't bear this in mind, you may develop misconceptions, which occasionally happened in Tibet.

At one time in Tibet, there were practitioners who denigrated and rejected Vajrayana because of their tremendous devotion to and focus on the vinaya, while others, because of their great admiration and enthusiasm for Vajrayana, neglected the practice of ethical discipline. If you understand Atisha's explanation of how the teachings of the Buddha are organized according to practitioners' different levels of mind, you will protect yourself from such grave errors.

2. *Every scriptural pronouncement without exception [will] dawn on your mind as a personal instruction.* The second greatness of the lam-rim is that all the teachings of the Buddha will "dawn on your mind as a personal instruction." If your understanding of the Buddha's teachings is limited, there is the danger that you will discriminate between the scriptures, regarding some as relevant to your practice and others as relevant only for academic study. If your understanding is more profound, how-

ever, you will realize that the way of the intelligent is to have an overview of the entire Buddhist path. This allows you to appreciate which teachings are relevant at a particular stage in your practice and which are not, while understanding that all the scriptures are instructions that will ultimately be relevant to your own personal practice at some point.

3. *Easy to discover what the Buddha intended.* The third greatness is that you will easily realize the Buddha's ultimate intention; that all the Buddha's teachings can actually converge in your practice. This will allow you to fulfill your spiritual aspirations, whatever they are—higher rebirth, liberation from cyclic existence [Skt: *samsara*] or complete enlightenment.

4. *Protect you…from the abyss of the great error.* The fourth greatness of the lam-rim is that it protects you from the "abyss of the great error," the great mistake of abandoning the Dharma. If you realize that all the Buddha's scriptures and teachings are relevant to your own personal practice, there is no room for discarding some and adopting others because you realize that actually, you need them all. Therefore, you will not abandon any of the Buddha's teachings.

This point also relates to the issue of sectarianism. Practitioners sometimes harbor sectarian sentiments because of differences between the four Tibetan Buddhist traditions. If you can understand the unique features of each tradition—their methods of approach, teaching and various types of practices—you will appreciate the value and importance of this variety. It is, in fact, possible for a single individual to integrate all these diverse teachings into his or her personal practice. As the Kadampa masters used to say, "One should know how to uphold the entire teaching of the Buddha, like lifting a square piece of cloth all at once."[17]

Some Mahayana practitioners make distinctions between the Lesser Vehicle and the Great Vehicle, tending to dismiss the Lesser Vehicle teachings, particularly the Theravada. One of the consequences of this is that Theravadins then begin to question the authenticity of the Mahayana tradition. In fact, however, the Pali tradition, from which the Theravada teachings arose, should be regarded as the source of the Mahayana as well, particularly the teachings on the Four Noble Truths and the thirty-seven aspects of the path to enlightenment.[18]

These are really the foundation and cornerstone of Buddhist practice. To these you add the practices of the six perfections and so forth in the manner of refining certain aspects of these foundational practices, and finally you add the practice of Vajrayana Buddhism. Therefore, even though you can add to it from the bodhisattva and Vajrayana teachings, the Pali canon is really a complete set of teachings in itself. Without the foundational teachings of the Lesser Vehicle, the Paramitayana and Vajrayana teachings are incomplete because they lack a basis.

QUESTION AND ANSWER PERIOD

Question. If there is a natural nirvana and a luminous, pure, fundamental nature, then what originally leads us to deviate from the pure luminosity for us to suffer from karma, defilements, obscurations and afflictions? How come we do not retain the state of pure luminous natural nirvana through the cycle of births and rebirths?

His Holiness. When Buddhism speaks of the luminous and fundamentally pure nature of mind, or consciousness, what is being suggested is that it is possible for the defilements to be removed from the basic mind, not that there is some kind of original, pure state that later became polluted by defilements. In fact, just as the continuum of our consciousness is without beginning, our delusions are also without beginning. As long as the continuum of consciousness has existed, so too has there been the continuum of delusion—the perception of inherent existence. The seeds of delusion have always been there together with the continuity of consciousness.

Therefore, Buddhist texts sometimes mention innate, or fundamental ignorance, which is spontaneous and simultaneous with the continuum of the individual. Only through the application of antidotes and the practice of meditation can these delusions be cleansed from the basic mind. This is what is meant by natural purity.

If you examine the nature of your own mind, you will realize that the pollutants, such as afflictive emotions and thoughts rooted in a distorted way of relating to the world, are actually unstable. No matter how powerful an affliction, when you cultivate the antidote of true insight into the nature of reality, it will vanish because of the power of the antidote, which undermines its continuity. However, there is nothing that can undermine the basic mind itself; nothing that can actually interrupt the continuity of consciousness. The existence of the world of subjective experience and consciousness is a natural fact. There is consciousness. There is mind. There is no force that can bring about a cessation of your mental continuum.

We can see parallels to this in the material world. According to Buddhism, the ultimate constituents of the macroscopic world of physical reality are what we call "space particles," which constitute the subtlest level of physical reality. It is on the basis of the continuum of these subtle particles that the evolution of the cosmos is explained. The universe evolves out of this subtlest level of physical reality, remains for a certain period of time, then comes to an end and dissolves. The whole process of evolution and dissolution arises from this subtlest level of physical reality.

Here we are talking about a perceptible and tangible world of physical reality that we can directly experience. Of course, in this world of everyday concrete reality, there will be forces that undermine its existence. The subtle level of physical reality, however, is regarded as something that is continuous—without beginning or end. From the Buddhist point of view, there is nothing that can bring an end to the actual continuum of the subtle level of reality.

Similarly, there are various manifestations of consciousness. These include the grosser levels of thought, emotion and sensory experience, whose existence is contingent upon a certain physical reality, such as environment and time. But the basic continuum of consciousness from which these grosser levels of mind arise has neither beginning nor end; the continuum of the basic mind remains, and nothing can terminate it.

If defilements had a beginning, the question would arise, where did they come from? In the same way, Buddhism does not posit a beginning to consciousness itself, because to do so raises more questions about what led to its creation. As to the question why there is no beginning of consciousness, one can argue for this on the basis of its ever-present continuum. The real argument, however, stems from a process of elimination, because if we posit a beginning of consciousness, what kind of beginning could it be and what could have caused it? Arguing for a beginning of consciousness undermines the fundamental Buddhist belief in the law of causality.

In some Buddhist texts, however, we find references to the Buddha Samantabhadra—the ever-good and ever-pure primordial Buddha. But here we have to understand the concept of primordiality in relation to individual contexts. In this understanding, the fundamental innate mind of clear light is seen as the original source of the macroscopic world of our experience. When the Vajrayana literature describes this evolution process, for example, it speaks of a reverse cycle and a forward cycle.

In both cases, the world of diverse consciousness and mental activity arises from a subtler level of clear light, which then goes through what is known as the "three stages of appearance." Through this process, there is an understanding that everything arises from this basic nature of clear light mind and is then dissolved into it. So again, our understanding is that this originality is in the context of individual instances, not some kind of universal beginning.

Question. Your Holiness, you spoke of monasteries like Vikramashila, where there was a strict code of ethics and where even highly realized masters could be expelled for breaking a vow. Today, certain rinpoches and high-level masters have been involved in different types of scandals. How come the code of ethics is different today?

His Holiness. One thing that needs to be clearly understood is that the individuals to whom you refer are no longer in the monastic order. People who have broken their vows, particularly one of the four cardinal rules—falsely proclaiming spiritual realizations, committing murder, stealing, and engaging in sexual intercourse—will automatically be expelled from the monastery. They will be expelled even if there are strong grounds for suspicion that they have broken their vows. This applies today as much as it did in the past. However, some of those who have broken their vows still find very skillful and devious means of retaining some kind of dignity and stature.

I always remind monks and nuns, therefore, that the moment they have transgressed their vinaya vows, they should no longer wear their monastic robes. This applies equally to members of all four schools of Tibetan Buddhism: Nyingma, Sakya, Kagyü and Geluk. Within the Tibetan tradition, however, there are two institutions of practitioners— the monastic institution of practitioners with monastic vows and the institution of lay practitioners, who wear different colored robes, don't shave their heads and have taken only lay precepts, or *pratimoksha* vows.

3

RELYING ON A SPIRITUAL TEACHER

THE QUALITIES OF A TEACHER

Lines of Experience: Verse 8

> Although (there is much merit to be gained from)
> reciting or hearing even once this manner of text (writ-
> ten by Atisha) that includes the essential points of all
> scriptural pronouncements, you are certain to amass
> even greater waves of beneficial collections from actu-
> ally teaching and studying the sacred Dharma (con-
> tained therein). Therefore, you should consider the
> points (for doing this properly).

Lama Tsong Khapa's *Lines of Experience* is a key to the connections and relationships between all the various scriptural texts. Verse 8 presents how the teacher should teach and how the students should listen, so that both teaching and listening are successful and effective. It is very impor-tant that the teacher has the right motivation and attitude. If the teacher is motivated by mundane aspirations, such as wanting to be known as a great scholar, to attract money or other material offerings or to bring people under his or her influence, then that teacher's motivation is cer-tainly polluted.

It is very important that a teacher's motivation for teaching be the pure, altruistic aspiration to be of service and benefit to others. According to traditional Tibetan teachings, not only should a teacher ensure purity of motivation but also the manner of giving the teaching should not be flawed. Teaching in a flawed way is likened to an old man eating; he chews only the soft food and puts the hard bits aside. Similarly, teachers should not just focus on the simple points and leave out the difficult ones. It is also said that teachers should not teach Dharma like crows build nests. When crows build nests, there is no systematic order; it's totally chaotic. Similarly, Dharma teachers should not teach chaotically but should offer a correct, systematic presentation that will benefit their students.

Another quality that ideally a teacher should have is experiential knowledge of the topic being taught. If that is not possible, then the teacher should have some familiarity with the practice of that topic, in order to be able to draw on personal experience. If that is not possible either, then at least the teacher should have a thorough intellectual understanding of the topic. As Dharmakirti said, there's no way that you can reveal to others that which is hidden to yourself.

I have a friend who is a great teacher and a very learned Hindu master. One day we were talking about the issue of inter-religious harmony and the need for greater communication among the different faiths. I remarked that I am completely ignorant on matters of Islam and don't have much contact with the Islamic world. He replied, "Well, it's not that difficult. Just learn to quote a few verses from the Koran and come up with some commentary here and there. That should be enough. You don't really have to know more."

A more serious example involves a German scholar who attended a discourse by a Tibetan teacher. During the discourse he heard things that contradicted some of the basic teachings of the Buddha, so after the lecture, he went up to the teacher in person and told him that it seemed he had made some mistakes. Instead of acknowledging these mistakes, the Tibetan teacher said, "Oh, it doesn't matter. You can say stuff like that." This is wrong; it's very important for teachers to be careful.

When giving teachings from a throne, teachers' physical conduct is also very important. Before sitting down, teachers should make three prostrations towards the throne. This is to remind them that teaching from a throne does not mean that they are being recognized as great or holy beings but rather reflects the respect that is being accorded to the Dharma being taught. According to the Mahayana tradition, when the Buddha gave the teachings on the perfection of wisdom, he himself made a throne to sit on in order to show respect for these sutras, which are considered to be the mother, or source, of all aryas, be they hearers, solitary realizers or fully enlightened buddhas.

When the Buddha's sutras were compiled by the early arhats and later by other followers of the Buddha, there were times when all the members of the congregation would remove their outer yellow robes. The person supervising the compilation process would fold and stack them up to make a throne and then sit on this throne of robes and compile the sutras. All this shows the tremendous respect accorded the Dharma.

Once the lama has sat down on the throne, the Tibetan custom is for him to recite a sutra reflecting on impermanence, to keep his motivation pure and prevent pride or conceit from arising in his mind. Such practices are important in ensuring purity on the teacher's part, because when you're sitting on a high throne and people start praising you, there's a real danger of pride and arrogance taking over.

Therefore, we should take to heart the instructions of the Tibetan master, Dromtönpa, who said, "Even if the whole world venerates you by placing you on the crown of their head, always sit as low as possible and maintain humility." In the *Precious Garland*, Nagarjuna makes aspirational prayers to be like the elements of earth, water, fire and wind, which can be enjoyed and utilized by all sentient beings. If you take such sentiments seriously, you will never think that you are better than others or to try to bring them under your control.

It is also very important to have pure motivation when you receive teachings; to ensure that you have the three qualities of the ideal student—an objective mind, intelligence and a deep interest in the teachings—and that you cultivate the appropriate attitude. In this way, you will become a suitable recipient of the teachings. You should regard the Dharma as a mirror and the actions of your body, speech and mind as what that mirror reflects. Constantly examine what you see in the mirror of Dharma and continually try to modify your behavior.

One feature of the Buddha's teaching is that the greater the diversity of your resources and avenues of contemplation, the more effective will be your understanding and experience, and the deeper the conviction you acquire. Therefore, you must ensure that your approach to your practice is comprehensive and that your learning and understanding are vast. At the same time, you must also ensure that the things you learn do not remain merely at the intellectual level. Right from the start, your studies should be directed towards the objective of practice. If you study without the desire to relate what you are learning to your own life through practice, you run the risk of becoming hardened or apathetic.

The great Kadampa masters used to say that if the gap between the Dharma and your mind is so big that a person can walk through it, your practice has not been successful. Make sure there's not the slightest gap between the teachings and your mind. You need to integrate and unite the Dharma with your mind. A Tibetan expression says that you can soften leather by kneading it with butter, but if that leather is hard because it's been used to store butter, you can never soften it, no matter how hard you try. Since you don't store butter in skin containers in the West, perhaps that saying doesn't make sense, but you get the idea.

The Kadampa masters also used to say that the water of Dharma can

moisten the earnest, fresh minds of beginners, no matter how undisciplined they are, but can never penetrate the minds of those hardened by
knowledge.

Therefore, learning and knowledge must never override your enthusiasm for practice, but neither should your dedication to practice interfere
with your commitment to study. Furthermore, both your knowledge and
dedication to practice must be grounded in a warm, compassionate heart.
These three qualities—scholarship, dedication to practice and compassion—should be combined.

If teachers and students prepare their minds as above, students can
experience transformation, even while listening to teachings.

Finally, at the end of each session, both the student and teacher
should dedicate their merit to the enlightenment of all sentient beings.

In the Tibetan tradition, there are two main ways in which a teaching
session can be conducted. In one, the primary objective is to help students gain a clearer understanding of the various philosophical points of
Dharma. In the other, the main emphasis is on specific aspects of the
individual's practice, where specific problems encountered in meditation
are addressed.

Broadly speaking, when great treatises such as the five major works
by Indian masters dealing with Middle Way philosophy are taught, the
primary objective is to help students gain deeper understanding and
clarity. However, when texts such as the lam-rim are taught, more
emphasis is placed on the practical application of specific meditation
practices, and instructions are given on a step-by-step basis.

There is also a unique style of teaching known as "experiential commentary," where the teacher teaches one specific topic at a time. The student then
practices this topic for a prolonged period of time, and only when the
student has had some experience will the teacher take him or her to the
next step. In this way, the teacher guides the student through an experi-

ential understanding of the subject matter.

Dromtönpa summarized the ideal qualities of a Mahayana teacher—profound resources of knowledge in all aspects of the Dharma, being able to draw on both sutra and tantra and explain the relationship between various ideas from different philosophical perspectives; the ability to see what is most effective for an individual student at any particular time; and the ability to recognize the particular approach most suited to a given individual.

THE PRACTICE OF RELIANCE

Lines of Experience: Verse 9

> (Having taken refuge,) you should see that the root cause excellently propitious for as great a mass of good fortune as possible for this and future lives is proper devotion in thought and action to your sublime teacher who shows you the path (to enlightenment). Thus you should please your teacher by offering your practice of exactly what he or she says, which you would not forsake even at the cost of your life. I, the yogi, have practiced just that. You who also seek liberation, please cultivate yourself in the same way.

From Verse 9 onwards, the main topic is the actual manner in which students are guided through the stages of the path. This is broadly divided into two sections. One is how to rely on the spiritual teacher, who is the foundation of the path, and the other is, having done that, how to engage in the actual practice of the stages of the path.

With respect to the former, Verse 9 explains the practice of proper reliance on a spiritual teacher [Skt: *kalyanamitra*; Tib: *ge-wai she-nyen*].

Just as there can be negative friends and spiritual friends, there can be both negative teachers and spiritual teachers.

With respect to ordinary, worldly knowledge, although in the final analysis what we learn comes through our own study and maturity of understanding, still, at the beginning, we need someone to introduce us to the subject matter and guide us through it. Similarly, when it comes to spiritual transformation, although true experiences come through our own development of knowledge and practice, we again need an experienced teacher to show us the path.

Since the spiritual teacher is so crucial to our practice, Lama Tsong Khapa goes into great detail in his *Great Exposition of the Stages of the Path*, presenting the topic in three broad categories: the qualifications of the spiritual teacher, the qualities required by the student and the proper teacher-student relationship.

THE QUALITIES OF THE SPIRITUAL TEACHER

The qualifications of a suitable teacher can be found in texts from the vinaya all the way up to the Vajrayana. Since here we are discussing Mahayana teachings in general, we will consider the ten qualifications of the teacher as presented in Maitreya's *Ornament of the Mahayana Sutras:*

1. A disciplined mind (referring to the quality of having mastered the higher training in ethical discipline).
2. A calmed mind (referring to the quality of having mastered the higher training in meditation and concentration).
3. A mind that is thoroughly calmed (referring to the quality of having mastered the higher training in wisdom, particularly the wisdom of no-self [Skt: *anatman*; Tib: *dag-med*]).
4. Knowledge exceeding that of the student in whatever subject is being taught.

5. Energy and enthusiasm for teaching the student.

6. Vast learning in order to have the resources from which to draw examples and citations.

7. Realization of emptiness—if possible, a genuine realization of emptiness, but at least a strong commitment to the practice of emptiness on the basis of deep admiration for the teachings on it.

8. Eloquence and skill in presenting the Dharma so that the teaching is effective.

9. Deep compassion and concern for the well-being of the student to whom the teaching is given (perhaps the most important quality of all).

10. The resilience to maintain enthusiasm for and commitment to the student, not becoming discouraged no matter how many times the teaching has to be repeated.

The first three qualities relate to the practice and experience of the Three Higher Trainings of morality, concentration and wisdom. The other important qualities are having the realization of emptiness as the ultimate nature of reality and compassion for the student. Those who assume the role of teacher must ensure that these qualities are present within themselves.

When discussing these ten qualities in his *Great Exposition of the Stages of the Path*, Lama Tsong Khapa makes a very important point. He says that if your own mind is not disciplined, there's no way you can discipline the mind of another.[19] Therefore, if you want to be a teacher, you must first seek to discipline your own mind. He goes on to say that the way prospective teachers should discipline their minds is through the practice of the Three Higher Trainings.

Furthermore, teachers should not be limited to teaching just one or two points of Dharma but should be able to present particular practices with complete knowledge of their place within the overall framework of the Buddha's teachings.

Lama Tsong Khapa concludes this section of his *Great Exposition* by emphasizing that practitioners seeking a spiritual teacher should familiarize themselves with these ten qualities and then look for them in those in whom they would entrust their spiritual welfare. When choosing a spiritual teacher, from the start, examine the person you have in mind to see if he or she really possesses these qualities. If you do so, you'll reduce the risk of encountering serious problems later on.

Otherwise, you may use the wrong criteria to judge a teacher's suitability. This used to happen in Tibet. Tibetans have tremendous faith in the Dharma, but their level of knowledge was not always equal to their devotion. Instead of assessing spiritual teachers by their inner qualities, people would base their judgment on external manifestations, such as the number of horses in a lama's entourage. If a lama was traveling in a large convoy, people would say, "Oh, he must be a *very* high lama!" People like that also tended to regard what the lama was wearing—a unique hat, brocade robes and so forth—as an indicator of his spiritual greatness.

It is said that when Atisha first came to Tibet, his translator, Nagtso Lotsawa, and the Ngari king, Jangchub Ö, sent letters inviting all the high Tibetan lamas to come and receive this great Indian master. A large procession of lamas came to meet Atisha, and as they rode up on horseback, they could be seen from quite a distance. They were all dressed in very impressive-looking costumes with elaborate headgear shaped into fantastic designs, such as crows' heads. When Atisha saw them, he covered his head with his shawl in mock terror and exclaimed, "Oh my! The Tibetan ghosts are coming!" When the lamas dismounted, they removed their brocades and costumes until they were wearing just their monastic robes, and walked towards Atisha, who then became very pleased.

On this subject, we can also look at the life of Milarepa, who shines as one of the crown jewels among Tibetan meditators. One day, the lama, Naro Bönchung, who had heard of Milarepa's great reputation, went to visit him. When he met Milarepa in person, however, he was taken completely by surprise, and later remarked to someone, "This Milarepa is so famous, but when you actually see him, he looks just like a beggar."

This reminds me of the humility of another great lama, the Kadampa master, Dromtönpa. The story goes that once, when Dromtönpa was traveling from one place to another, he met a Tibetan monk who had been walking for some time. This monk was very tired and his boots had begun to hurt his feet, so he took them off and, since Dromtönpa looked like just a humble layman, asked him to carry his boots. Dromtönpa took the heavy boots on his back without question. Later, as they approached a monastery, the monk noticed that all the monks were lined up on both sides of the road, obviously waiting to receive somebody. He thought to himself, "They didn't know I was coming, and anyway, this reception could not possibly be for me," so he turned to Dromtönpa and said, "This welcome is obviously for someone important. Do you have any idea who it's for?" Dromtönpa replied, "It could be for me." The monk looked at him in astonishment and, realizing what he had done, ran off, leaving his boots behind.

There is also a much more recent example. Around the turn of the century, there was a great meditation master and teacher named Dza Patrul Rinpoche, who was truly a great bodhisattva and embodied the teachings of Shantideva's text, *A Guide to the Bodhisattva's Way of Life*. Dza Patrul Rinpoche had many disciples but often led the life of a wandering practitioner. Whenever he settled in one area, he would begin to attract disciples and particularly patrons. After a while, he would find it all too much and go elsewhere to seek solitude.

One of those times, Dza Patrul Rinpoche sought shelter in the home of an old lady, and started doing household chores while pursuing his spiritual practice. One day, as he was outside emptying the lady's chamber pot, some lamas stopped by the house. They told the old lady that they had heard their teacher might be residing somewhere in the region and asked if she had seen him. She asked what he looked like, and as they started to describe his general appearance, the kind of clothes he wore and so forth, she suddenly realized that the person who was outside emptying her pot was the great Dza Patrul Rinpoche. She was so embarrassed that, just like the monk in the previous story, she too ran off. I heard this story from the late Khunu Lama Tenzin Gyaltsen.

The point of all this is that a true Mahayana teacher should be someone who enjoys simplicity, yearns to be anonymous and, as Tibetans would say, hides in solitude like a wounded animal. The Tibetan tradition states that Mahayana teachers should have at least two basic qualities. First, from the depths of their heart, they should regard the future life as more important than this. Without this, nothing one does becomes Dharma. Second, teachers should regard the welfare of others as more important than their own. Without this, nothing one does becomes Mahayana.

THE QUALITIES OF THE STUDENT

In his *Great Exposition,* Lama Tsong Khapa goes on to discuss the three principal qualifications of an ideal student:

1. An objective and open mind.
2. The intelligence to judge between right and wrong, appropriate and inappropriate.
3. Enthusiasm for and interest in the subject.

Objectivity and openness are critical, regardless of what you want to study. Bias is an obstacle to knowledge. Objectivity ensures that you are engaging in the Dharma in the right way and with the right motivation. The sutras and Nagarjuna's *Precious Garland* both emphasize this and describe four wrong ways of approaching and engaging in the Dharma:

1. Engaging in the Dharma out of attachment to a particular tradition or custom.
2. Engaging in the Dharma out of hatred or hostility.
3. Engaging in the Dharma to seek temporary relief from some actual or perceived threat.
4. Engaging in the Dharma out of ignorance.

With respect to the second point, sometimes people have so much aversion to something that they embrace whatever opposes it. For example, there are people in India who are motivated to engage in the Dharma in rebellion against their traditional caste status as untouchables. They embrace Buddhism because of negative feelings towards their traditionally inherited religion.

The second quality of the ideal student, intelligence, is also very important, since it is intelligence that allows you to discriminate between right and wrong and so forth.

When commenting on this quality and the various attitudes that practitioners must have towards their teacher, Lama Tsong Khapa writes that students should relate to their teachers as loyal and respectful children. This does not mean that you should give your leash to anybody who is willing to take it, but only to one who possesses the right qualifications. To substantiate this point, he cites a vinaya sutra that says that if a teacher says something that contradicts the Dharma, you should not follow that teaching. Another passage states that if a teacher says something contradictory to the overall framework of the Buddha's path, the student must point this error out to the teacher.

This reminds me of a story. The Tibetan master and learned schol-ar, Geshe Sherab Gyatso, used to attend the discourses of one of his teachers, Muchog Rinpoche. Whenever Muchog Rinpoche made some effective point, Geshe Sherab would immediately praise it and say, "Yes, these are powerful instructions. Deeply inspiring." However, if Muchog Rinpoche said something contradictory to the teachings of the Buddha, Geshe Sherab would immediately rebuff what his teacher had said, say-ing, "No, no, no. Nobody should say such things."

With respect to the third quality of the student, enthusiasm for and interest in the teachings, right at the beginning of the *Great Exposition of the Stages of the Path*, when Lama Tsong Khapa states his intention for writing the text, we find a request for the attention of readers who have the quality of objectivity, are endowed with the faculty of intelligence and wish to make their human existence meaningful. In order to make your life meaningful, you need enthusiasm for and interest in practicing the teachings, otherwise, whatever you learn is like the drawing of a lamp—it doesn't illuminate anything—and your knowledge remains at the level of mere information.

We find similar exhortations among the Indian masters. In the salu-tation verses of his commentary on Maitreya's *Ornament of Clear Realization*, Haribhadra states that his teacher, Vimuktisena, wrote a commentary on the *Perfection of Wisdom Sutras*. Vasubandhu, Vimuktisena's own teacher, had also written a commentary on these sutras, but interpreted their ultimate meaning according to Cittamatra philosophy. Recognizing that his teacher, Vasubandhu, hadn't fully understood the meaning of these sutras, Vimuktisena wrote his own commentary as a corrective. This shows that even students with great devotion and respect for their teacher should have the intelligence to point out any mistakes their teacher makes.

Another example concerns the Indian master, Dharmakirti, whose teacher was a student of the seventh century pandit, Dignaga. Dharmakirti used Dignaga's text in his study of epistemology. As he read over the text with his teacher, Dharmakirti realized that even his own teacher hadn't fully understood Dignaga's meaning. When Dharmakirti mentioned this to his teacher, he invited him to write a commentary that would take his own interpretation as an object of critique.

All these examples show clearly that the great masters truly took to heart the Buddha's own advice that his followers should not accept his words simply out of reverence but should scrutinize them in the way a goldsmith examines gold by rubbing, cutting and scorching and accept the validity of his teachings only on the basis of their own analysis.[20]

The Mahayana has a long tradition of subjecting the Buddha's words to detailed analysis and examination, following that with an interpretative approach to discriminate between teachings that can be taken at face value and those that require further interpretation.[21] This is necessary because there are certain scriptural teachings that, if taken literally, actually contradict reasoning and experience. These interpretations have been made by Mahayana practitioners and masters who have unwavering, single-pointed faith in the Buddha, some of whom have actually been willing to give up their lives in the service of the Dharma. Even such devoted masters subject the word of the Buddha to critical analysis.

ESTABLISHING PROPER RELIANCE

In his *Great Treatise*, Lama Tsong Khapa goes on to describe the actual manner in which proper reliance on a spiritual teacher should be developed and established. "Reliance on a spiritual teacher," he writes, "is the foundation of the path, because the spiritual teacher is the source of all temporary and (particularly) ultimate gain." The point here is that if we encounter a genuine spiritual teacher, this person may be able to help us open our eye of awareness and lead us on the path.

The actual practice of relying on a spiritual teacher is performed through both thought and action, but relying through thought is the key. This entails the cultivation of two principal qualities, faith and respect. In the lam-rim, we often find citations from Vajrayana texts stating that we should perceive our teacher as a truly enlightened being. It is important to understand the significance of this practice.

By encouraging you to cultivate a perception of your teacher as an enlightened being, the lam-rim texts do not mean that such reliance on a spiritual teacher is indispensable. If you look at the structure of the lam-rim teachings, although all the practices are organized within the framework of the three scopes, those of the initial and middling scopes are regarded as common practices, the term "common" implying that they are not full or complete practices in and of themselves.

The *initial scope* teachings discuss the need to cultivate the yearning for a better rebirth and contain practices related to that aspiration. The *middling scope* teachings deal with the practices of the Three Higher Trainings of morality, meditation and wisdom, but even here they are not presented in full because they are still in the context of the Mahayana path. The point is that lam-rim texts are written assuming that the ultimate aim of the practitioner is to enter the Vajrayana path in order to reach enlightenment (the *great scope*). Therefore, even though the lam-rim teachings present the idea of perceiving your teacher as a truly enlightened being, it does not mean that every single spiritual practice depends upon that kind of reliance. Cultivating the perception of your teacher as a fully enlightened being is relevant only in the context of Vajrayana but not in the common practices.

The actual reliance on a spiritual teacher is done through the cultivation of certain thoughts, particularly faith, admiration and respect, based on the recognition of your teacher's great kindness. It does not end there, however. In fact, the very purpose of cultivating such attitudes is to arouse enthusiasm for and dedication to your practice. By cultivating such thoughts as admiration and respect, you develop a deeper appreciation of what your spiritual teacher embodies, and your commitment and dedication to practice naturally increase. The best way of making an offering to your teacher is to practice what you have been taught. As Milarepa wrote, "I do not have any material things to offer my teacher, but still I have the best offering—my practice and experiences."

Among the writings of the great masters we find a verse stating that while there might be a question as to whether single-pointed meditation can lead you to liberation, there is no doubt that deep faith in, devotion to and respect for your teacher will. This suggests that if, in the context of Vajrayana, you have deeply felt, single-pointed faith in and respect for your spiritual teacher, you will experience enormous enthusiasm and make great strides in your practice.

The Indian Chakrasamvara master, Gandapa [Tib: Drilbupa], wrote that your spiritual teacher alone can lead you to liberation. However, commenting on this point, Lama Tsong Khapa said that the term "alone" here is not exclusive but rather an emphasis placed upon the importance of relying on your spiritual teacher in the context of Vajrayana. Devotion to your teacher does not exclude the necessity of all the other practices, because devotion alone cannot lead to liberation. You need to understand the different contexts in which certain perspectives are relevant. If you have a broad understanding of the whole idea of reliance on a guru, it will help you deal with some of the problems and crises we see today in relation to this practice.

QUESTION AND ANSWER PERIOD

Question. If I did not misunderstand what you said before, part of the practice of guru devotion is to point out where you think your teacher has gone wrong. First, what do you do when it is nearly impossible to express a dissenting opinion to your teacher because those around him or her tend to block the expression of criticism? Second, how do you reconcile holding fundamentally different views on certain issues from those expressed by your guru?

His Holiness. If a lama or spiritual teacher has done something wrong that needs to be pointed out, there could be two kinds of motivation for those immediately around the teacher—such as attendants or close disciples—trying to hide it or prevent people from disclosing it or pointing it out to the teacher. On the one hand, their motivation could be quite innocent; they might just be trying to protect and help their teacher. Such motivation is more the result of ignorance rather than willful manipulation of the situation. However, even if that's the case, there is still the danger of causing harm to the teacher. In fact, a Tibetan expression says that extremely devout students can turn a true teacher into a false one.

On the other hand, the motivation of the attendants and close disciples could be more mundane—they may not want to make their teacher's wrongdoing public for fear of harming his or her reputation. This is completely wrong, and you must find a way of expressing your concerns to your teacher. However, it is also very important to ensure that your own motivation is pure. You should not act out of hostility towards your teacher or out of the desire simply to express your displeasure. As the Mahayana teachings state, we must ensure that everything our teacher teaches accords with the principal teachings of the Buddha. We must also practice the motto of relying on the teaching and not the person.[22]

In response to your second question, it's unlikely that you will have disagreements with your teacher on every single issue. That's almost impossible. Basically, you should embrace and practice the teachings that accord with the fundamental teachings of the Buddha and disregard those that do not.

Question. Do we need a guru to get enlightened or is it sufficient just to study Dharma, live a moral life, attend teachings and practice meditation?

His Holiness. Of course it is possible to practice, study and lead a moral life without actually seeking a guru. However, you must understand that when you talk about enlightenment, you are not talking about something that can be attained within the next few years but about a spiritual aspiration that may, in some cases, take many lifetimes and eons. If you do not find a qualified teacher to whom you can entrust your spiritual well-being then, of course, it is more effective to entrust yourself to the actual Dharma teachings and practice on that basis.

I can tell you a story related to this. Dromtönpa was a great spiritual master who truly embodied the altruistic teachings of exchanging self and others. In fact, in the latter part of his life, he dedicated himself to serving people who suffered from leprosy. He lived with them and eventually lost his own life to this disease, which damaged his chin in particular.

As Dromtönpa lay dying, his head rested on the lap of one of his chief disciples, Potowa, and he noticed that Potowa was crying. Then Potowa said, "After you pass away, in whom can we entrust our spiritual well-being? Who can we take as our teacher?" Dromtönpa replied, "Don't worry. You'll still have a teacher after I'm gone—the tripitaka, the threefold collection of the teachings of the Buddha. Entrust yourself to the tripitaka; take the tripitaka as your teacher."

However, as we progress along the spiritual path, at some point we will definitely meet an appropriate and suitable teacher.

Question. Many texts describe the practitioner's goal as that of buddhahood itself, yet among seasoned Western Dharma teachers there seems to be a trend towards accepting partial results, as if buddhahood is unattainable. This new attitude is that of accepting samsaric mind punctuated by spiritual phases and seems to be based on those diligent teachers' inability to achieve complete liberation themselves. Is seeking buddhahood in this very lifetime still a viable goal in what the Buddha declared would be a dark age for Buddhism?

His Holiness. If you understand the process of attaining buddhahood from the general Mahayana perspective, the attainment of buddhahood within the period of three countless eons is actually said to be the quick version. Some texts speak about *forty* countless eons! However, according to the general Vajrayana teachings, practitioners with high levels of realization can prolong their lifespan and attain Buddhahood within a single lifetime. The Highest Yoga Tantra teachings recognize that even within this short human lifetime, the possibility of full enlightenment exists.

There is also the idea of someone being able to attain full enlightenment after a three-year retreat, which is not too dissimilar from Chinese communist propaganda. I make this comment partly as a joke, but partly in all seriousness—the shorter the time period of your expectation, the greater the danger of losing courage and enthusiasm. Leaving aside the question of whether it takes three or forty countless eons to reach enlightenment, when you cultivate deeply such powerful sentiments as those articulated in Shantideva's prayer,

> For as long as space exists,
> For as long as sentient beings remain,
> Until then, may I too remain
> And dispel the miseries of the world,

time is totally irrelevant; you are thinking in terms of infinity. Also, when you read in the Mahayana scriptures passages pertaining to the bodhisattva's practice of what is called armor-like patience, again time has no significance. These are tremendously inspiring and courageous sentiments.

4

BECOMING INSPIRED TO PRACTICE DHARMA

Lamp for the Path: Verse 2

> Understand that there are three kinds of persons
> Because of their small, middling and supreme capacities.
> I shall write clearly distinguishing
> Their individual characteristics.

Having explained how to rely on a spiritual teacher, in his *Great Exposition*, Lama Tsong Khapa goes on to discuss the procedure for engaging in the practices of the path. This is divided into two sections: how to inspire ourselves with enthusiasm for practice and how to actually engage in it. To practice Dharma successfully, we need determination and courage. We can arouse these qualities within ourselves by reflecting upon the preciousness of our human existence in three ways:

1. Recognizing the opportunities our human existence affords us.
2. Appreciating the rarity of these opportunities.
3. Appreciating the great significance of these opportunities.

Once we have been inspired and have developed a determination to

engage in the practice of Dharma, there are three main objectives that
we seek:

1. The attainment of a higher rebirth in future lives.
2. The attainment of liberation from cyclic existence.
3. The attainment of full enlightenment.

There are three types of path leading to these three spiritual goals and,
as we have seen, the lam-rim teachings present them within the framework of the three scopes. The main practice that fulfills the aspirations
of the initial scope—avoiding the three lower realms and attaining a
higher rebirth—is that of maintaining the ethical discipline of refraining from the ten non-virtuous actions: killing, stealing, sexual misconduct, lying, divisive speech, harsh speech, meaningless gossip, covetousness, harmful intent and wrong views. This practice is undertaken on
the basis of a clear recognition of the karmic law of cause and effect.

These ten actions encompass all the various negative manifestations
of body, speech and mind. The practice of the ten *virtuous* actions is to
maintain an ethical discipline where you deliberately and consciously
refrain from the ten non-virtuous ones. If you engage in such an ethical
discipline, you will establish the conditions for attaining a favorable existence in your next life.

The main practice that fulfills the aspirations of the middling scope—
liberation from cyclic existence—is that of the Three Higher Trainings.

The main practice that fulfills the aspirations of the great, or highest, scope—the full enlightenment of buddhahood—is that of the six
perfections, which is undertaken on the basis of generating the altruistic mind that aspires for enlightenment for the benefit of all beings—
bodhicitta—which we discussed briefly earlier.

Just as there are different methods that need to be cultivated on each
of these paths, there are also different factors that need to be overcome

and eliminated. For example, in the context of the first spiritual goal of attaining a higher rebirth, the main factors that need to be overcome are the negative manifestations of the afflictions, such as the non-virtuous actions of body, speech and mind. In the context of the second spiritual goal of attaining liberation, the main factors that need to be overcome are the mental and emotional afflictions that lie at the root of our suffering. In the context of the third spiritual goal of attaining enlightenment, the main factors that need to be overcome are the subtle imprints left on our consciousness by the afflictions, which obstruct us from gaining perfect knowledge, the omniscient mind of buddhahood.

Lamp for the Path: Verse 3

> Know that those who by whatever means
> Seek for themselves no more
> Than the pleasures of cyclic existence
> Are persons of the least capacity.

The "means" in the first line refers to the practice of taking refuge in the Three Jewels, which includes reflecting on death and its inevitability and following the law of karma.

This verse goes on to define the characteristics of the initial scope (calling it "least capacity"), referring to practitioners who aspire to the first spiritual goal of attaining higher rebirths in cyclic existence and therefore lead ethically disciplined lives, refraining from the ten non-virtuous actions based on a deep conviction in the truth of the law of karma.

DEVELOPING FAITH IN KARMA

According to Buddhist tradition, the subtlest workings of karma are evident only to the omniscient minds of the buddhas; ordinary beings have no way of understanding karma at its deepest levels. Therefore, in order to be deeply convinced of the truth of the law of karma, you need to have a deep conviction in the validity and efficacy of the Three Jewels of Refuge; the basis of your spiritual practice must be strong faith in Buddha, Dharma and Sangha.

This faith is not developed from the words of the Buddha alone but, as we have seen, on the basis of your own critical analysis. If you look at the Buddha's teachings, you can discern two basic objectives: the secondary, temporary objective is to help sentient beings gain upper rebirths, but the primary, ultimate objective is to lead them to complete liberation from samsara.

When you examine the Buddha's teachings on the complex issue of negative emotions and how to counter them, you can see that these matters are evident to all. We are all familiar with the emotions, so as we relate the Buddha's teachings on them to our own personal experience, we can gradually recognize the truth of the Buddha's words. Similarly, all his teachings dealing with the ultimate goal of liberation—impermanence, the Four Noble Truths, emptiness and so forth—can also be understood through critical analysis. That analysis can then be extended to the scriptures dealing with the subtle workings of karma. We can thus conclude that if Buddha has not failed us in the most important area, the attainment of liberation, why should he fail us in his teachings on cause and effect? In this way we can begin to develop conviction in the law of karma. We can also consider that the Buddha had no reason to make false claims about karma and how there are no contradictions in the scriptures discussing it.

To summarize, once we develop a deep conviction in the validity of the Buddha's teachings, we gain an admiration for and faith in the Buddha himself. Based on these considerations, we can recognize the validity of the Buddha's teachings on karma. It is on this basis that we then engage in the practice of ethical discipline, refraining from the ten non-virtuous actions.

The Three Levels of Refuge

If there is a threat, we should seek refuge from it. Similarly, in the context of spiritual practice, to protect ourselves from the threat of an unfavorable rebirth, we should seek refuge in the Three Jewels: Buddha, Dharma and Sangha.

Buddhism teaches three different levels of refuge. The first is where we seek protection from the immediate threat of the suffering of rebirth in a lower realm of existence. Inspired by the great fear that this possibility evokes, we seek refuge in the Three Jewels in order to avoid it. This level of refuge is relevant to initial scope practitioners, whose goal is to attain an upper rebirth.

When we think of the lower realms of existence, we should not think of some place far away in the distant future. All that actually lies between the present moment and the next life is simply the continuity of our breath. The moment we stop breathing, when we breathe out and don't breathe in, the next life is right there in front of us. It's not a matter of some distant time in the future; it's immediate. In order to bring about a concordant sense of urgency, therefore, it is necessary for us to reflect upon impermanence, particularly upon the inevitably of death, the uncertainty of the time of death and what will benefit us when death arrives.

The second level of refuge is where we seek protection from the suffering of pervasive conditioning; the suffering of being caught in cyclic existence and the destructive power of the negative thoughts and emotions. In order to overcome these sufferings, we take refuge in Buddha, Dharma and Sangha, which embody the total transcendence of suffering and cyclic existence, particularly the suffering of pervasive conditioning. This level of refuge is relevant to middling scope practitioners, whose goal is to attain nirvana.

The third and highest level of refuge is that of the Mahayana practitioner. Here, we seek refuge from the extremes of samsaric existence on the one hand and individual liberation on the other. In order to be protected from these two extremes, we seek the attainment of buddhahood, dharmakaya and rupakaya, for the benefit of all sentient beings. When we view refuge in this way, we can understand the significance of Maitreya's statement that the true and ultimate refuge is Buddha alone, because only an enlightened being embodies all this perfection. Maitreya goes on to say that the Buddha's enlightened mind encompasses the ultimate jewel of Dharma and also represents the ultimate perfection of the jewel of Sangha.

THE VALUE AND TRANSIENT NATURE OF HUMAN EXISTENCE

Lines of Experience: Verse 10

> This human existence with its (eight) liberties[23] is much more precious than a wish-granting jewel. Obtained just this once, difficult to acquire and easily lost, (it passes in a flash) like lightning in the sky. Considering how (easily this can happen at any time) and realizing that all worldly activities are as (immaterial as) chaff, you must try to extract its essence at all times, day and night. I, the yogi, have practiced just that. You who also seek liberation, please cultivate yourself in the same way.

This verse presents the contemplations that need to be done to fully appreciate the significance of the opportunities offered us by our human existence. First, we must recognize the nature of this existence; second, we must reflect upon its rarity; and third, we must consider its fragility; the fact that it can be lost at any time. Based on such contemplations, we should then reflect upon these three important facts:

1. Death is inevitable.
2. The time of death is unpredictable.
3. At the time of death, only spiritual practice will be of benefit.

Most of us feel that we will be alive tomorrow. We think that just because there are no medical or physical conditions threatening our lives, we can justifiably conclude that there is a ninety-nine percent chance that we will live beyond today. However, what about that one percent? We cannot say with one hundred percent certainty that we won't be dead tomorrow. When death strikes, our wealth, no matter how great, will be of no significance; nor will our family or friends. Even our cherished body will be of no use. At the time of death, nobody else can help us; we must travel that path alone.

Now the big question arises: does the continuity of consciousness disappear after death? This is an important question and not new to this generation; it has been addressed for thousands of years. However, when actually confronted by death, only the spiritual qualities we have developed through our practice of Dharma will help; nothing but Dharma can benefit us at the time of death.

MEDITATION: CULTIVATING MENTAL DISCIPLINE

The way we develop positive qualities of mind is through constant practice and meditation. Meditation is a discipline whereby we cultivate familiarity with a chosen object. Our problem is that in normal day-to-day life, we allow ourselves to be dominated by afflictive emotions and deluded thoughts, totally overwhelming our mind with negative states that then perpetuate a whole cycle of problems, confusion and suffering.

What we seek in spiritual practice, therefore, is a way of reversing this cycle so that we can finally take charge of our mind and prevent it from coming under the influence of such negative impulses. We do this by engaging in a constant discipline of cultivating familiarity with a chosen object, which, of course, must be a positive one. In so doing, we gain a certain mental stability that allows us to place our mind single-pointedly upon this object. This is the actual meaning and purpose of Buddhist meditation.

Thoughts and emotions with which we are more familiar are the ones that come more easily to us. If we are more familiar with negative thoughts and emotions, those are the ones that will arise in us more naturally, but if we are more habituated to positive thoughts and emotions, those are the ones that will naturally arise.

We can observe this in our own personal experience, particularly when studying a new subject. At the beginning, we find it difficult and struggle to understand anything at all, but as we persevere, the clearer it becomes. Eventually we reach the point where understanding arises through merely directing our mind to the subject. This does not mean that the subject has suddenly become easy. All we have done is to enhance our understanding of it through constant engagement.

Change is a gradual process. Therefore, when we are trying to dispel confusion with respect to reality, illumination dawns by degrees. Again, we can observe this in our personal experience. At the beginning, we may have a single-pointed perception of reality that is completely opposite to the way in which things really exist, but as we investigate the nature of reality with our analytical mind, we eventually reach the point where our misconceptions are undermined and we enter a state of uncertainty. We still tend more towards misconception, but our grasping at it has been loosened. As we continue deepening our understanding through our analysis, our indecisiveness gradually progresses into a state of equilibrium, where we begin to incline more towards the correct understanding of reality.

As we further deepen our understanding through investigation and critical thinking, we reach the point where we have a clear intellectual understanding of reality, having convinced ourselves that this is the way in which things actually exist; that this is the true nature of reality. If we deepen our analysis even further, we gain even stronger conviction; a certainty derived from our own critical thinking. This is called "valid cognition"; a true ascertainment of a certain state of affairs.

If we pursue this process of constantly engaging our mind with the object—in this case, the nature of reality—we reach the point where we have not only intellectual, inferential knowledge of the object but also a kind of experiential knowledge. At this initial stage, the experience still depends to a large extent upon rational thought processes and is therefore called the stage of "simulated experiential knowledge."

If we continue deepening our analysis, we reach the point where our experiential knowledge becomes spontaneous and we can recall the experience of deep understanding simply by focusing our attention on the object of investigation. At this point, our understanding has reached the level of "spontaneous, non-simulated experiential knowledge." Thus, even with a single characteristic of phenomena, our thought processes go through deepening levels of understanding and experience.

From another point of view, we can say that we go through three stages of understanding. First, there is the understanding derived from learning and study; from listening to teachings, for example. Second, there is the stage of understanding derived not so much from learning and study, but from personal reflection and contemplation. Third, there is the level of understanding that derives from personal experience; from meditation.

There are two principal approaches to the actual process of meditation. One is called "placement" or "absorptive meditation"; sometimes this is also called "calm abiding." The other is "analytic" or "insight meditation." Let's take the example of meditating on cultivating faith in your spiritual teacher or another high object, such as the Buddha.

Initially, you can cultivate a firm, deeply grounded, genuine faith in your teacher by, for example, constantly reflecting upon his or her great qualities from various points of view. The more resources you can draw upon in this analytic meditation, the stronger will be your feeling of connectedness to your teacher.

Once you have arrived at the point where from the depths of your heart you feel reverence, admiration and closeness, let your mind abide in this state. This is placement meditation. As you remain single-pointedly in this feeling of admiration for your teacher, the intensity and vitality of this state may slowly begin to diminish. When you observe this happening, reinforce your awareness by reapplying your analytic meditation on your teacher's positive qualities.

When you engage in meditation on impermanence or no-self nature, you take impermanence or no-self as the object of your attention and focus on it, trying to deepen your understanding of it. Here again, you engage in analytic meditation by constantly reflecting upon the various reasons that led you to the conclusion that all phenomena are impermanent or not self-existent. When you arrive at the conclusion that everything is definitely impermanent or definitely lack self-existence, place your mind single-pointedly on that conclusion. Abide as long as you can in that state of absorptive meditation.

These examples show how analytic and absorptive meditations combine to make a successful meditation session.

If you think about your own daily experiences, you will see that you engage in analytic and absorptive meditation all the time. For example, your thoughts are constantly influenced by strong emotions, such as attachment to somebody you like or anger towards somebody you don't. When you are attached to somebody, you're always thinking how desirable that person is and examining that person's positive, attractive qualities, constantly justifying, reinforcing and dwelling in your feelings of attachment. Similarly, when you feel strong aversion towards somebody, you constantly reinforce your hatred by thinking up one reason after another to justify your feelings—"he did this," "she didn't do that" and so forth—and abide in these feelings. Thus, you are already familiar with practices similar to analytic and absorptive meditation.

As spiritual practitioners, what we should be doing is applying the experiences with which we are familiar to a realm that is not—that of spiritual practice. Through the application of analytic and absorptive meditation we can really bring about the spiritual transformation that we seek. There is, however, a third condition that we may have to take into account.

Take, for example, two practitioners under the guidance of the same teacher, who have both studied and practiced meditation for an equal length of time. One finds it easy to understand the teachings and is very successful in gaining realizations, but the other finds it difficult, even though he or she has put in an equal amount of time, attention and effort.

Buddhism explains this in terms of merit or a lack thereof—a person's karma and level of karmic obscuration. For example, those who support themselves through wrong livelihoods[24] will have much heavier degrees of karmic obscuration than those who don't. Some people who have devoted their whole life to solitary meditation have told me that when they utilize offerings from certain people, it temporarily hinders their progress. This suggests that because of the purity of their way of life, they have developed an extremely fine-tuned sensitivity to environmental factors and can immediately recognize the effect of things on their practice.

In summary, three factors contribute to a successful meditation practice:

1. Successful engagement in analytic and absorptive meditation.
2. Accumulation of merit and purification of negativity and karmic obscurations.

3. Engagement in specific meditation practices for particular purposes.

Of the three, engagement in specific meditation practices is the most important and is done in the meditation session, whereas other virtuous activities, such as making prostrations, circumambulating and so forth are done in the post-session periods.

During the actual session, the faculty of introspection ensures that you continually maintain mindfulness and are not distracted by external factors. And while introspection and mindfulness are critical during the session, they are also very important during the post-meditation periods, when they ensure that you sustain the vitality and diligence of your meditation experiences.

You must also ensure that during the post-meditation periods you carry out your normal activities, such as eating, sleeping and so forth, in an appropriate manner, that is with mindfulness and introspection. If you do, the practices you did during the session will reinforce and enhance those of the post-meditation periods and the practices you do during the post-meditation periods will reinforce and enhance those of the session. If you can maintain your spiritual practices effectively in this manner, their influence may even extend into your sleep, and mindfulness and introspection will function in your dreams as well. You may, for example, experience powerful surges of admiration for the Buddha or your spiritual teacher in your dreams and be able to feel the lingering effects of such experiences even after you awaken.

Finally, to ensure the quality of your meditation practice, it is more effective to do many short sessions rather than a few long ones.

DEATH AND REBIRTH

As to what specific meditation practices you should engage in, take the topic of impermanence as an example. The significance of meditating on impermanence and death is not just to terrify yourself; there is no point in simply making yourself afraid of death. The purpose of meditating on impermanence and death is to remind you of the preciousness of the opportunities that exist for you in life as a human being. Reminding yourself that death is inevitable, its time unpredictable and when it happens only spiritual practice is of benefit gives you a sense of urgency and enables you to truly appreciate the value of your human existence and your potential to fulfill the highest of spiritual aspirations. If you can develop this profound appreciation, you will treat every single day as extremely precious.

As spiritual practitioners, it is very important for us to constantly familiarize our thoughts and emotions with the idea of death so that it does not arrive as something completely unexpected. We need to accept death as a part of our lives. This kind of attitude is much healthier than simply trying not to think or talk about death. When we examine the teachings of the Buddha himself, we find that during his first public sermon he enumerated sixteen characteristics of the Four Noble Truths, of which four are the characteristics of suffering. Of the four characteristics of suffering, the first is impermanence. Then, when the Buddha passed away, at the threshold of his final nirvana, the last teaching he gave was on the importance of contemplating impermanence. In other words, the very first and last teachings of the Buddha were on impermanence.

A discussion of death naturally brings up the question of what happens next, bringing up the issue of rebirth. From the Buddhist point of view, rebirth is understood in terms of a continuity of consciousness. One of the premises of the Buddha's teachings on rebirth, therefore, is the continuity of consciousness. In his *Pramanavarttika*, Dharmakirti states that something that is not in the nature of consciousness cannot be turned into consciousness. His point is that in accounting for the nature and existence of consciousness, we have two choices. Either we posit that the continuum of consciousness has no beginning or that it does. If we posit a beginning to the continuum of consciousness, the question arises, when did that first instance of consciousness come into being and from where did it come? Then our choices are that the first moment of consciousness came from nowhere—from no cause—or that it was created by a cause that is permanent and eternal.

From the Buddhist point of view, either answer gives rise to many inconsistencies. If something comes from no cause, it should exist either all the time or not at all. Both options are untenable. If, on the other hand, something comes from a cause that is itself permanent, eternal, unchanging and unitary, this negates the fundamental Buddhist view of universal causation. Therefore, from the Buddhist point of view, the idea of divine creation is completely unacceptable. If one accepts that some divine force created the entire universe, then the nature of this divine force has to be independent, unitary, uncaused and original, all of which are untenable within a philosophical outlook in which universal causation is the fundamental principle.

It is on these grounds that Buddhists do not posit a beginning to the continuum of consciousness and explain its nature and existence purely in terms of the principle of causes and conditions. From the Buddhist point of view, even the existence of the galaxies and the universe itself has to be explained from the point of view of causes and conditions. In the case of the universe, there has to be a relationship between the sentient beings that inhabit the physical plane and the existence and evolution of the physical world.

Buddhists explain it in the following way. As I mentioned before, at the subtlest level of the physical world, there is an ever-present physical continuum of space particles. When this subtle physical continuum interacts with the karma of sentient beings, the karma acts as a condition that gives rise to various permutations of physical reality. Eventually there comes into being a macroscopic world that can actually have a direct effect upon sentient beings' experience of pain, pleasure, suffering and happiness. It is along these lines that Buddhists explain the entire evolution and dissolution of the universe. This is made very clear in the traditional Buddhist teachings on the twelve links of dependent origination.[25]

THE TWELVE LINKS

The interlocking chain of the twelve links demonstrates the entire process of evolution and explains the individual's existence in samsara. There is no concept of there being some kind of central, unifying creator around which everything evolves.

While we are experiencing the consequences of one set of twelve links, the ignorance and karmic action links of another cycle have already been set in motion. Thus, there are ever-rotating, interlocking chains of twelve links of dependent origination constantly keeping us bound to the wheel of life, which is how our evolution through cyclic existence is explained.

The Buddha actually taught the twelve links in two ways. One charts our evolution through cyclic existence from ignorance to karmic volitional acts to consciousness and so on down the chain, while the other presents the same process in reverse, explaining how we escape from samsara and reach enlightenment. By bringing an end to ignorance, volitional acts are prevented; by preventing volitional acts, consciousness is prevented, and so on.

Commenting on these teachings, the Indian master Asanga identified three principal features:

1. Everything has its causes. In the Buddhist teachings on dependent origination, the notion of divine creation is

rejected, because everything comes into being as a result of causes and conditions.

2. These causes are impermanent. Even the causes that set the whole cycle in motion are themselves subject to causes and conditions and are, therefore, impermanent.

3. Only compatible and corresponding causes give rise to the effects. Causation is not a random process; not everything can produce everything. Causes and effects must be compatible; only commensurate causes lead to corresponding results.

Asanga identified these factors by commenting on a passage from the sutras, where the Buddha stated, "Because this exists, that exists; because this originated, that will ensue; and because there is fundamental ignorance, volitional acts will follow."[26]

5

REFUGE, KARMA AND PRECEPTS

TAKING REFUGE

Lines of Experience: Verse 11

> After death, there is no guarantee that you will not be
> reborn in one of the three unfortunate realms.
> Nevertheless, it is certain that the Three Jewels of
> Refuge have the power to protect you from their ter-
> rors. For this reason, your taking of refuge should be
> extremely solid and you should follow its advice with-
> out ever letting (your commitments) weaken.
> Moreover, (your success in) so doing depends on your
> considering thoroughly which are the black or the
> white karmic actions together with their results and
> then living according to the guides of what is to be
> adopted or rejected. I, the yogi, have practiced just
> that. You who also seek liberation, please cultivate
> yourself in the same way.

Here, the text points out that the answer to the question of where you will
go after death is determined by your own karmic actions, not only of this
life but also of your previous lives. On this point, Vasubandhu has written
that since all of us have enormous collections of karma accumulated over

many past lives, we all have karmic potentials to take rebirth in the lower realms of existence as well as in the more fortunate realms.

What factors determine which karmic collection will ripen first? Vasubandhu said that the strongest, or most dominant, karmic collection, will ripen first. If your positive and negative karma are of equal strength, then the karmic actions to which you are most habituated will ripen next. If the level of familiarity of your karmic actions is also equal, then the karma that will ripen next is whichever you accumulated first.[27] This is how karma determines your future rebirths and whether, for example, you will be reborn in one of the three lower realms, that is the hell, hungry ghost [Skt: *preta*] or animal realms. Although explanations of these unfortunate realms of existence may be found in abhidharma texts such as Vasubandhu's *Treasury of Manifest Knowledge (Abhidharmakosha),*[28] you should investigate the descriptions of the location and nature of these realms to see how literal and accurate they are.

The second sentence of Verse 11 reads, "Nevertheless, it is certain that the Three Jewels of Refuge have the power to protect you from their terrors." This obviously refers to the practice of taking refuge in the Three Jewels: Buddha, Dharma and Sangha. To take refuge, two conditions must be present—fear of rebirth in the three lower realms and faith in the power of the objects of refuge to protect you from this threat.

Therefore, to take refuge successfully, you must have some understanding of what these objects of refuge are. As Buddhist practitioners, we must first understand the possibility of there being such a thing as a Buddha, and also the possibility of enlightenment. The key factor here is an understanding of the nature of Dharma, because Dharma is the actual refuge. Once you understand the nature of Dharma, you can also understand the possibility of Sangha and its perfected state, the Buddha.

Generally speaking, we do not want to experience fear, apprehension or anxiety. However, fear is a complex emotion involving many factors. There is one category of fear or anxiety that is totally groundless and is born from

an over-active imagination or some kind of paranoia or overly suspicious
mind. This kind of fear is completely unnecessary and needs to be eliminated. Then there is another type of fear, which stems from encountering a
real threat. If there is no possibility of overcoming this danger and you have
to face it no matter what, fear is not an appropriate response and is, in fact,
quite pointless; all it does is paralyze you.

However, the type of fear that arises because you are alert to a particular danger can also motivate you to act—for example, to seek protection or escape. This type of fear is not only justified; it can be positive and beneficial. This is the kind of fear you need in order to take
refuge properly. We deliberately cultivate a sense of fear of rebirth in the
three lower realms, and this inspires us to seek refuge from this danger.

The text speaks about having a "solid" refuge in the Three Jewels;
this means a refuge that is stable and firm. The key thing in developing
a stable and firm practice of refuge is a good understanding of dependent origination and, to a certain extent, emptiness. By contemplating
the teachings on dependent origination and emptiness, you will see
clearly the possibility of buddhahood. In this way, you will gain a deep
understanding of the nature of Dharma and a recognition of Sangha and
Buddha. Once you have developed full confidence in the power of
Buddha, Dharma and Sangha to protect you from the suffering of the
three lower realms and entrusted them with your spiritual care, your
refuge is solid and you have truly become a practicing Buddhist.

If, however, your confidence in the Three Jewels weakens and
doubts about their ability to protect you arise, you can no longer claim
to be a true practitioner of Buddhadharma.

OBSERVING THE LAW OF KARMA

Once you have taken refuge in the Three Jewels, your main responsibility is to observe the law of karma and abstain from the ten negative

actions. Verse 11 concludes: "Moreover, (your success in) so doing depends on your considering thoroughly which are the black or the white karmic actions together with their results and then living according to the guides of what is to be adopted or rejected. I, the yogi, have practiced just that. You who also seek liberation, please cultivate yourself in the same way."

There are different kinds of karmic actions and various ways of categorizing them. Since we all share the same fundamental nature, which is the natural aspiration to be happy and not to suffer, actions leading to happiness are generally considered to be positive, or virtuous, while actions leading to pain and suffering are generally considered to be negative, or non-virtuous. Therefore, it is in their causal relationship to happiness and suffering that the distinction between positive and negative, or virtuous and non-virtuous, actions is made. With respect to the medium through which these positive and negative actions are created, we have actions of body, speech and mind.

Karmic acts involve multiple factors, such as initial motivation—the state of mind that impels an action—object of the action, execution of the act itself and state of mind on completion of the act. The nature of the karma created by an action differs depending upon whether these factors are virtuous, neutral or non-virtuous during the four stages. There can be thoroughly non-virtuous actions and thoroughly virtuous actions, but also actions that are partly virtuous and partly non-virtuous, and actions that are neutral as well.[29]

The law of karma falls within the general law of causality. What distinguishes the karmic law of cause and effect from the more general one is the involvement of sentient beings. The law of karma refers to a causal nexus within which a sentient being acts with intelligence and motivation. This motivation sets certain actions in motion, which then lead to certain causations and results.

In discussing karma, therefore, the multiple factors such as motivation, execution of the act and so forth mentioned above must be taken into account. All these factors play a role in determining the nature of the karma created. Whenever a karmic act occurs, be it physical, verbal or mental, the act itself lasts only until its completion, but its consequences can arise much later on. Certain karmas ripen during the life in which they were created, others in the very next life and the rest in subsequent lifetimes. An important question in Buddhist philosophical discourse asks what is the factor that links the initial karmic act to its fruition? To explain this, there is the notion of karmic "propensities," or "imprints," which means that even though an act is over once it has been completed, its imprint, or potentiality, remains.

There is much discussion in the Buddhist literature on the question of where this imprint is stored. Many Buddhist thinkers maintain that karmic propensities are stored and carried in the consciousness. When we look at the teachings on the twelve links of dependent origination, we find that fundamental ignorance gives rise to volitional acts; karma leaves an imprint on the consciousness; and consciousness gives rise to the subsequent links. Therefore, in this context, it is consciousness that is the repository of karmic imprints.

However, there are times in one's existence when one is totally devoid of conscious activity, such as when a meditator is completely absorbed in single-pointed meditative equipoise on the direct realization of emptiness. In that state, not a single part of the person's mind is polluted, because the meditator is in a state of uncontaminated wisdom. At such times, where could the karmic traces reside?

One of the most profound answers to this question is that the imprints are maintained simply on the basis of the mere sense of I that we all naturally have. This mere I is the basis of the imprints left by the karma that created them and is the link between the initial execution of the act and its fruition at a later stage. This issue is discussed extensively in Nagarjuna's *Fundamentals of the Middle Way.*

Lines of Experience: Verse 12

> The fullest strides (of progress) in actualizing the
> supreme paths will not come about unless you have
> attained the working basis (of an ideal human body)
> that is complete with (all eight ripened favorable) qual-
> ities. Therefore, you must train in the causal (virtuous
> actions) that will preclude (your attainment of such a
> form) from being incomplete. (Furthermore) as it is
> extremely essential to cleanse away the stains of black
> karmic debts and downfalls (from broken vows) tar-
> nishing the three gateways (of your body, speech and
> mind), and especially (to remove) your karmic obsta-
> cles (which would prevent such a rebirth), you should
> cherish continually devoting yourself to (applying) the
> complete set of four opponent powers (which can
> purge you of them). I, the yogi, have practiced just
> that. You who also seek liberation, please cultivate
> yourself in the same way.

As I mentioned before, when we reflect upon the potential of our
human life and the opportunity it affords us of attaining the highest
spiritual aspiration of full enlightenment, we will realize the preciousness of our human existence, particularly that which is endowed with all
favorable conditions. Therefore, we read in Verse 12, "The fullest strides
(of progress) in actualizing the supreme paths will not come about
unless you have attained the working basis (of an ideal human body)
that is complete with (all eight ripened favorable) qualities." The eight
favorable qualities, or conditions, include longevity, physical attractive-
ness, high family, great wealth and power, trustworthy speech, fame and
strength of body and mind.

The eighth favorable condition is birth as a male, but this needs to be understood in its proper context, because the ultimate aim of human existence is to attain full enlightenment with its omniscient wisdom. Should the opportunity to do this during a particular culture or era be greater as a female, this favorable condition would be reversed. Without this perspective, you might consider this point to be sexist.

PURIFICATION OF NEGATIVE KARMA: THE FOUR OPPONENT POWERS

We then read, "(Furthermore) as it is extremely essential to cleanse away the stains of black karmic debts and downfalls (from broken vows) tarnishing the three gateways (of your body, speech and mind), and especially (to remove) your karmic obstacles (which would prevent such a rebirth), you should cherish continually devoting yourself to (applying) the complete set of four opponent powers (which can purge you of them)." With respect to refraining from negative actions in the future, you can determine to maintain an ethical discipline that will protect you from committing negative acts in future, but what about the negative actions you have already committed? The only way to deal with these is to purify them.

There is a Tibetan saying, "If there's one good thing about negativities, it's that they can be purified." However, there are different degrees of purification. One possibility is to completely eliminate the potency of a karmic act such that it can never ripen at all. Another is to diminish the gravity of a serious negative karma such that its fruition will be less damaging. A third possibility is to delay the fruition of a negative karma that cannot be entirely purified.

The text refers to the four opponent powers that should be used when practicing purification:

1. The power of regret, or repentance.
2. The power of reliance.

3. The power of virtuous activity.

4. The power of resolve.

Of these four, the most important is the power of repentance. From the depths of your heart, you must feel a deep sense of regret for the negativities you have created, as if you had ingested poison.

The second power is that of reliance. If you look at the many negative actions you have created, most of them are related to either higher beings, such as the Buddha, or fellow sentient beings. Therefore, you practice the power of reliance by taking refuge in the Three Jewels and generating bodhicitta, feeling strong compassion for all sentient beings.

Third is the power of engaging in virtuous acts specifically aimed at purification. Whenever you engage in a virtuous act, you can direct it towards the purpose of purifying your negative karma. In the Tibetan Buddhist tradition, the general custom is to engage in practices specifically associated with purification, of which six are often cited: reciting the names of buddhas, especially in the bodhisattva's confession sutra with prostrations to the Thirty-five Buddhas;[30] reciting certain mantras, especially the one hundred syllable Vajrasattva mantra and the mantra of Vajra Akshobhya (Mitukpa);[31] reciting sutras; meditating on emptiness; making offerings; and commissioning the creation of images.[32]

The fourth power is a deep sense of resolve that you will not indulge in such negative actions in the future, even at the cost of your life. During this practice, you may be aware that you might not be successful in completely abstaining from all of these negative actions or from a particular negative act, but while you are actually practicing purification, you should generate the strong determination that you will not indulge in such acts in future.[33]

QUESTION AND ANSWER PERIOD

Question. If a person is struck by an illness and commits an act of murder, what can that person do to purify his or her karma?

His Holiness. If by "illness" you mean some kind of psychological or emotional disturbance that leads to insanity, then from the Buddhist ethical point of view, such an act carries less karmic weight than a premeditated murder committed with full knowledge of the consequences. It is also lighter than a murder committed out of powerful negative emotions, which, again from the Buddhist ethical point of view, is also considered a complete act of murder.

Whatever the nature of the non-virtuous act, however, the practice you should do to purify the negative karma is universal and must contain the four opponent powers. When you practice the power of regret, remember the being against whom the act was directed and, employing all four powers, engage in virtuous acts, such as profound meditation on bodhicitta or emptiness. There are also general purification practices that apply in such cases as well. If you are not capable of cultivating the four powers and engaging in an act of purification, an alternative is simply to recite mantras or engage in some other positive act with the intention of purifying the karmic deed.

Question. With our knowledge of karma and the effect of good and bad deeds, how would a Buddhist society treat criminals?

His Holiness. From the Buddhist point of view, it is important to distinguish between the act and the individual who commits it. You can totally reject the act but you must maintain compassion towards the individual who did it, always recognizing the person's potential for transformation and correction. Whatever method that society uses as a corrective means needs to be applied. However, the individual needs to be corrected in such a way that he or she learns to recognize that what they did was wrong; that it was a negative act. It is only on the basis of such recognition that correction can truly begin. From the Buddhist point of view, therefore, the death penalty is out of the question. Even the idea of life imprisonment is problematic, because it, too, fails to recognize the possibility of correction.

6

SEEKING FREEDOM FROM CYCLIC EXISTENCE

RENUNCIATION

Lamp for the Path: Verse 4

> Those who seek peace for themselves alone,
> Turning away from worldly pleasures
> And avoiding destructive actions
> Are said to be of middling capacity.

In this reference to turning away from worldly pleasures, we have to understand that according to Buddhism, even things and events that are conventionally regarded as pleasurable are ultimately all *dukkha,* that is they are of the nature of suffering and dissatisfaction. When the Buddha explains the path that transcends suffering, he is referring not only to painful experiences but also to conventionally pleasurable ones. This understanding is not unique to Buddhism, but common to both Buddhist and non-Buddhist schools in India.

We can see this by looking at some of the meditation practices found in non-Buddhist traditions, particularly those aimed at cultivating the four levels of concentration. The fourth level of concentration, in particular, is said to be a state where, for the meditator, pleasurable and painful experiences no longer exist. Then, of course, the higher levels of the four formless absorptions are also beyond any sensations of pain or pleasure.[34] Even though some non-Buddhist schools accept that one needs to transcend even pleasurable sensations, the unique understanding of Buddhism is that the *very condition* upon which these experiences arise is also of the nature of suffering and therefore the basis of dissatisfaction.

"Destructive actions" means all karmic actions that perpetuate the cycle of conditioned existence; practitioners of middling capacity generate the genuine aspiration to seek freedom from it. They seek to engage in a path that undercuts the process generated by fundamental ignorance and to reverse the whole causal nexus of ignorance, volitional karmic acts and their subsequent sufferings. All the practices related to this spiritual goal are common to practitioners of middling capacity, the term "common" indicating that these practices are preparatory, or preliminary, stages for the Mahayana practitioner.

When practitioners cultivate the recognition that the emotional and mental afflictions are the true enemy and that underlying them is fundamental ignorance, they then engage in the methods for eliminating this ignorance. Practitioners recognize that as long as they remain under the control of the afflictions, they will never be free of dissatisfaction and suffering. If, based on this recognition, practitioners then generate a genuine and deeply felt aspiration to seek liberation from this bondage, that is true renunciation. This is a sentiment and practice unique to the Buddhist path.

UNDERSTANDING THE NATURE OF CYCLIC EXISTENCE

Lines of Experience: Verse 13

> If you do not make an effort to think about true sufferings and their drawbacks, you will not properly

develop a keen interest to work for liberation. If you do
not consider the stages whereby (true) origins of all suffering place and keep you in cyclic existence, you will
not know the means for cutting the root of this vicious
circle. Therefore, you should cherish exuding total disgust and renunciation of such existence by knowing
which factors bind you to its wheel. I, the yogi, have
practiced just that. You who also seek liberation, please
cultivate yourself in the same way.

The sufferings referred to in the first sentence are the three levels of suffering. The first is the suffering of suffering—the obvious and evident
painful experiences and sensations that we all experience. The second is
the suffering of change; the third, the suffering of pervasive conditioning.
In the context of cultivating true renunciation, we are really looking at the
third category—the suffering of pervasive conditioning, which refers to
the simple fact that our existence is controlled by fundamental ignorance
and the afflictions to which it gives rise. As long as we are bound by these
afflictions, there's no room for any lasting happiness. It is crucial, therefore, that we develop a deeply felt recognition of the afflictions as our true
enemy; without it, we will not develop a genuine aspiration to seek freedom from them.

The Sanskrit term *bhagavan*, which is sometimes translated into
English as *lord*, as in Lord Buddha, has the connotation of someone who
has conquered and gone beyond the state of negativity and limitation.
"Conquered" refers to the Buddha's victory over the four "demons," or
obstructive forces [Skt: *mara*]:

1. The afflictions [Skt: *klesha mara*].
2. Death (caused by conditioned existence) [Skt: *marana mara*].
3. The five aggregates (conditioned existence itself) [Skt:
   skandha mara].

> 4. The obstacles to overcoming the previous three, the "divine
> youth demon" [Skt: *devaputra mara*].

Of these four obstructive forces, the main one is the afflictions. A buddha is someone who has totally overcome, or conquered, these four
maras.[35]

There are both gross and subtle forms of the four maras, as there are
gross and subtle obscurations. The subtle are explained in terms of the
subtle obscurations to knowledge [Skt: *jneyavarana*; Tib: *she-drib*].[36]

Actually, the obstructive, or demonic, forces are the afflictions and anything that voluntarily embraces them, and when the afflictions and virtue
come into conflict and we take the side of the afflictions, we ourselves run
the risk of becoming a part of the obstructions. Also, if somebody willing-
ly and enthusiastically embraces the afflictions and relishes the experience
of having them in his or her life, that person will see practitioners trying
to combat their own destructive, negative emotions as misguided or
even crazy. Such a person, too, becomes a part of the obstructive forces.
As Tibetan masters like to say, "Negative friends don't necessarily appear
with horns on their heads." Negative friends are simply those who interfere with the spiritual practice of others.

If, then, you have a deeply felt recognition of the afflictions as the
true enemy, the aspiration will naturally arise within you to free yourself
from them and gain liberation. However, simply having the aspiration
to be free is not enough. You also need to develop an understanding of
whether such freedom is possible and whether you can cultivate it within yourself.

The afflictions and the karmic actions they produce are the cause of
suffering; underlying them is fundamental ignorance. You need to develop a deep understanding of how the cause of suffering actually leads to
its result. If you do not understand how cyclic existence comes into
being and how its sufferings arise, then even though you may want to

gain freedom, you won't be able to understand how it can come about. Then you might become disheartened, because although you realize the nature of your bondage, you can't see the possibility of release.

There are many subtleties in the nature of fundamental ignorance, the ultimate cause of the afflictions and suffering, but basically, it is a flawed perception of our own existence and the world around us. The subtlest explanation of fundamental ignorance is that it is the mind that grasps at the true, inherent existence of our self and all other phenomena. We gain complete liberation by eliminating this fundamental ignorance from its root.

There are grosser levels at which we can understand no-self, such as the absence of the person as some kind of autonomous agent. Grasping at the self as an autonomous agent serves as a basis for other afflictions such as attachment and hostility, which can be eliminated, but true liberation can only occur by eradicating the subtlest grasping at self. Therefore, the text reads, "If you do not consider the stages whereby (true) origins of all suffering place and keep you in cyclic existence, you will not know the means for cutting the root of this vicious circle. Therefore, you should cherish exuding total disgust and renunciation of such existence by knowing which factors bind you to its wheel."

There are two key elements in the practice of renunciation—the cultivation of a sense of disillusionment with cyclic existence and an understanding of the causal mechanism of the origin of suffering. When you have generated this combination of disillusionment and understanding, you can envision the possibility of freedom. With this, you will experience a sense of joy, because not only can you see the possibility of release; you also have the confidence that there exists a path by which you can attain it.

It is in this context of the practice of the middling scope that the teachings of the Four Noble Truths are explicitly relevant. As we discussed earlier, the Four Noble Truths encapsulate the essence of the unique teaching of the Buddha. Lama Tsong Khapa, in both the *Great* and *Middling Exposition(s) of the Stages of the Path*, observed that the principle of the Four Noble Truths has been repeatedly stressed in many scriptures, both Mahayana and non-Mahayana, and that through the teachings on the Four Noble Truths, we can develop a deep understanding of the process of causation in both samsaric and liberated existence. Therefore, Lama Tsong Khapa recommends that teachers impart to their students an understanding of the path on the basis of the Four Noble Truths.

The process of causation of the Four Noble Truths is explained in greater detail in the teachings of the twelve links of dependent origination, which we discussed earlier [see page 81]. It is possible to contemplate these teachings at three different levels. On one level, we can contemplate the twelve links in relation to the process of taking rebirth in the three lower realms, beginning from fundamental ignorance obscuring the true nature of reality, which leads to the volitional negative acts that precipitate lower rebirths.

We can also contemplate the twelve links in relation to cyclic existence in general, because even positive karma can give rise to rebirth in cyclic existence. Finally, it is possible to contemplate the twelve links specifically in the context of the subtle obscurations to knowledge, where although the individual may have gained freedom from the afflictions, there is still continuity in physical, or conditioned, existence.

When we think of liberation, we should not feel that it exists somewhere outside of us, like some physical domain. Liberation has to be understood in terms of our own state of mind. We have already mentioned natural nirvana—the natural purity in all of us that serves as the basis of true liberation once all the afflictions have been eliminated [see pages 16 ff.]. When we go deeper into the meaning of the nature of liberation, or *moksha*, therefore, we understand it in terms of the ultimate nature of our own mind when all afflictions have been removed.

What lies at the root of our unenlightened[37] existence is our fundamental misconception of the ultimate nature of reality. Therefore, by cultivating correct insight into true nature of reality, we begin the process of undoing unenlightened existence and set in motion the process of liberation. Samsara and nirvana are distinguished on the basis of whether we're in a state of ignorance or wisdom. As the Tibetan masters say, when we're ignorant, we're in samsara; when we develop wisdom, we're liberated. The ultimate antidote for eliminating fundamental ignorance is the wisdom realizing emptiness. It is this emptiness of mind that is the final nirvana.

Therefore, our ignorance of emptiness as the fundamental nature of reality, our ignorance of the emptiness of mind, is what traps us in cyclic existence, and knowledge of the emptiness of mind is what will set us free.

The Buddha taught the path that enables us to eliminate the afflictions and gain liberation on the basis of the Three Higher Trainings. The direct antidote to fundamental ignorance is the wisdom realizing no-self, the wisdom realizing emptiness. This does not refer to a mere cognition of emptiness but to a heightened realization where we can experience emptiness *directly*.

To have such a direct and powerful experience of emptiness, we need single-pointed concentration. That's why we need the higher training in concentration, or meditation. To progress in the higher training in concentration, we need to observe the ethical basis—the higher training in morality.

The practice of morality enables us to accumulate merit and purify negativity, but in the context of the Three Higher Trainings, its main purpose is to develop mindfulness and introspection. When we lead an ethically disciplined life, we are constantly applying these two faculties. As we sharpen our mindfulness and introspection, we lay the foundation for the successful realization of single-pointed concentration. The practices of morality, concentration and insight are all essential. The sequence is also definite: first, morality; then, meditative concentration; then, insight into emptiness.

QUESTION AND ANSWER PERIOD

Question. You said that emotional afflictions are the causes of suffering. Can we remove our afflictions without removing our emotions?

His Holiness. Definitely. For example, one of the antidotes to emotional afflictions is meditation on emptiness. As we deepen our experience of emptiness, we get a powerful surge of emotion, which itself acts to counter the negative, or afflictive, emotions. We also find in Buddhist practice specific antidotes to specific problems. For example, we meditate on loving kindness to counter hatred and hostility, and on impermanence to counter strong attachment. In other words, the emotion of love is generated as an antidote to anger and the experience of impermanence as an antidote to attachment.

One difference between the destructive, negative emotions on the one side and constructive, positive emotions on the other is that constructive, positive emotions have a strong grounding in valid experience and reasoning. In fact, the more we analyze these positive emotions, the more they are enhanced. Negative, afflictive emotions, by contrast, are usually quite superficial. They have no grounding in reason and often arise out of habit rather than reasoned thought processes.

Question. Does love dilute pain and suffering in the same way that light dispels darkness?

His Holiness. Perhaps the parallel is not that close, because light dispels dark directly and instantaneously; darkness vanishes the moment you switch on a light. The effect of love on pain and suffering is more complex and indirect. When we cultivate love and compassion, they promote within us strength and courage, allowing us to be more tolerant and able to bear hardship. This is how love helps us deal with and overcome pain and suffering. It's an indirect relationship.

7

CULTIVATING THE ALTRUISTIC INTENTION OF BODHICITTA

Lamp for the Path: Verse 5

> Those who, through their personal suffering,
> Truly want to end completely
> All the suffering of others
> Are persons of supreme capacity.

This verse refers to those practitioners who generate compassion and loving kindness towards others on the basis of a deep understanding of the nature of their own suffering. They understand that suffering comes into being as a result of the mental afflictions rooted in fundamental ignorance and recognize that as long as they are under the control of these afflictions and the underlying ignorance, sufferings will continue to arise ceaselessly, like ripples on a lake.

Once you understand the nature of suffering in relation to your own existence in this way, you can extend your understanding to see that all sentient beings suffer from bondage by the afflictions. Reflecting on their suffering, you then cultivate the insight that just as you yourself want to be free from suffering, so do they. This is how you begin to cultivate great compassion. When you generate the wish for all sentient beings to be happy, this is the start of loving kindness.

On the basis of compassion wishing others to be free of suffering and loving kindness wishing others to be happy, you then generate a sense of special responsibility. Your compassion does not remain simply at the level of a wish or aspiration. You generate a sense of commitment: "I *myself* shall liberate all beings from suffering." Eventually, this extraordinary sense of responsibility leads to the realization of bodhicitta—the altruistic intention of one who aspires to attain buddhahood for the benefit of all sentient beings. Thus, there are two kinds of aspiration in the realization of bodhicitta: the aspiration concerned for the welfare of all sentient beings and the aspiration to attain buddhahood for their sake.

The spontaneous intention to attain buddhahood for the benefit of all sentient beings occurs when these two aspirations are complete. This is the realization of bodhicitta, the mind of enlightenment. At this point, the student has become a practitioner of the highest capacity and all activities and practices motivated by bodhicitta are those of the Greater Vehicle, the Mahayana.

Lines of Experience: Verse 14

> Ever-enhancing your enlightened motive of bodhicitta is the central axle of the Mahayana path. It is the basis and foundation for great waves of (enlightening) conduct. Like a gold-making elixir, (it turns) everything (you do) into the two collections, (building up) a treasure of merit gathered from infinitely collected virtues. Knowing this, bodhisattvas hold this supreme precious mind as their innermost practice. I, the yogi, have practiced just that. You who also seek liberation, please cultivate yourself in the same way.

The first sentence describes bodhicitta as the central axle of the Mahayana path. Bodhicitta is a truly courageous and remarkable sentiment and the basis of the entire bodhisattva practice. The terms "basis" and "foundation" in the next sentence mean that the moment you have realized bodhicitta, you have become a Mahayana practitioner and are on the path to complete enlightenment but the moment your bodhicitta degenerates, you fall outside the fold of the bodhisattvas. Without bodhicitta, no matter how advanced you are in other practices—even if you have a direct realization of emptiness or have attained nirvana—nothing you do becomes the conduct of a bodhisattva or the cause of enlightenment.

The third sentence refers to an elixir that transforms base metals into gold. This means that with bodhicitta, even a seemingly insignificant act of virtue, such as giving food to an ant, is transformed into a condition for attaining full enlightenment. It then mentions "infinitely collected virtues," which indicates the expansiveness of this altruistic intention. Bodhicitta is a mind concerned with the welfare of infinite sentient beings. It enables us to commit to working for their benefit for infinite eons and motivates us to engage in an infinite variety of skillful means to help them.

Thus, bodhisattvas are referred to as enlightened "heroes" or "warriors." They are highly altruistic beings who have the wisdom to realize that by dedicating themselves to the welfare of other sentient beings, the fulfillment of their own self-interest comes automatically as a by-product. They are also heroic in the sense that they have dedicated their lives to attaining total transcendence and victory over the four obstructive forces. The verse concludes, "Knowing this, bodhisattvas hold this supreme precious mind as their innermost practice. I, the yogi, have practiced just that. You who also seek liberation, please cultivate yourself in the same way."

Lamp for the Path: Verse 6

> For those excellent living beings
> Who desire supreme enlightenment,

I shall explain the perfect methods
Taught by the spiritual teachers.

This verse refers to practitioners who have gained a degree of experience of compassion and bodhicitta and participate in ceremonies in order to affirm and stabilize these qualities. Verses 7 through 18 describe the entire ceremony for reinforcing and affirming the generation of the altruistic intention of bodhicitta.

Lamp for the Path: Verses 7 to 18

7. Facing paintings, statues and so forth
   Of the completely enlightened one,
   Reliquaries and the excellent teaching,
   Offer flowers, incense—whatever you have.

8. With the seven-part offering
   From the *[Prayer of] Noble Conduct,*
   With the thought never to turn back
   Till you gain ultimate enlightenment,

9. And with strong faith in the Three Jewels,
   Kneeling with one knee on the ground
   And your hands pressed together,
   First of all take refuge three times.

10. Next, beginning with an attitude
    Of love for all living creatures,
    Consider beings, excluding none,
    Suffering in the three bad rebirths,
    Suffering birth, death and so forth.

11. Then, since you want to free these beings
    From the suffering of pain,
    From suffering and the cause of suffering,
    Arouse immutably the resolve
    To attain enlightenment.

12. The qualities of developing
    Such an aspiration are
    Fully explained by Maitreya
    In the *Array of Trunks Sutra*.

13. Having learned about the infinite benefits
    Of the intention to gain full enlightenment
    By reading this sutra or listening to a teacher,
    Arouse it repeatedly to make it steadfast.

14. The *Sutra Requested by Viradatta*
    Fully explains the merit therein.
    At this point, in summary,
    I will cite just three verses.

15. If it possessed physical form,
    The merit of the altruistic intention
    Would completely fill the whole of space
    And exceed even that.

16. If someone were to fill with jewels
    As many buddha fields as there are grains
    Of sand in the Ganges
    To offer to the Protector of the World,

17. This would be surpassed by
    The gift of folding one's hands
    And inclining one's mind to enlightenment,
    For such is limitless.

18. Having developed the aspiration for enlightenment
    Constantly enhance it through concerted effort
    To remember it in this and also in other lives,
    Keep the precepts properly as explained.

THE IMPORTANCE OF BODHICITTA

The highest perfection of altruism, the ultimate altruism, is bodhicitta complemented by wisdom. Bodhicitta—the aspiration to bring about the welfare of all sentient beings and to attain buddhahood for their sake—is really the distilled essence, the squeezed juice, of all the Buddha's teachings, because ultimately, the Buddha's intention is to lead all sentient beings to perfect enlightenment, complete omniscience. Since it is bodhicitta that determines whether or not our practice becomes the path to enlightenment, bodhicitta is truly the heart essence of all the teachings of the Buddha. Thus, all 84,000 discourses of the Buddha can be seen as either preliminary to the practice of bodhicitta, the actual practice of bodhicitta, or precepts and activities in which we must engage as a result of taking the bodhicitta pledge.

When we come to recognize all this, we will really appreciate the preciousness of our human existence, which gives us the ability to reflect on and express the limitless qualities of bodhicitta. Similarly, when we reflect upon the kindness of the spiritual teacher who introduces us to bodhicitta and explains its nature and benefits, we will develop a deep sense of admiration and gratitude towards our Dharma guide.

The altruistic intention is important not only at the beginning of the path but also while we are on it and even after we have attained full enlightenment. As Shantideva pointed out, even before we have entered the path and do not have a genuine realization of bodhicitta but only an intellectual understanding of it and admiration for what it represents, this alone brings us immediate benefit. Regardless of how much we are under the control of the afflictions, we receive this benefit the moment we are able to appreciate the value of bodhicitta. However, the joy and serenity we experience come mixed with a sense of sadness for the fate of other sentient beings.

On the path, the practice of bodhicitta helps expedite our accumulation of merit. It also serves as the basis for the successful development of all the subsequent practices. It is like an all-in-one method, enabling us to purify quickly all our accumulated negative karmic imprints. Finally, when we become buddha, it is bodhicitta that sustains the never-ending continuity of our enlightened activity dedicated to the welfare of all sentient beings. Reflecting on this, we will truly appreciate the importance of bodhicitta, which benefits us at all stages of our spiritual path, and will clearly understand why it is compared to a wish-granting jewel.

In the Vajrayana tradition, there are unique methods for attaining the two enlightened holy bodies of rupakaya and dharmakaya. The main method for attaining the rupakaya, the buddha-body of form, is the perfection of skillful means, the method aspect of the path. This primarily refers to the altruistic intention to attain buddhahood for the benefit of all sentient beings, particularly the intention to attain the form body of a buddha in order to benefit and serve others. Without this aspiration, we cannot realize the full profundity of the Vajrayana path in cultivating the conditions for attaining the rupakaya.

Also, without the altruistic aspiration, the wisdom realizing emptiness does not have the potency to prepare us to cultivate the conditions for attaining the dharmakaya, the buddha-body of reality. Thus, the entire Vajrayana path can be seen as a series of practices arranged to enhance the ideals and aspirations of bodhicitta. Without bodhicitta, the Vajrayana path has no depth.

Leaving aside the issue of Buddhism or religious faith, we can see even from our own day-to-day experiences that the more we cultivate altruism and a sense of caring for others, the greater the immediate benefits we ourselves receive. Not only do we sleep better at night but also, regardless of whether we believe in the law of karma or not, the actions we create become more positive, constructive and virtuous.

If, on the other hand, we harbor ill-will, are self-centered and lack concern for others, not only do we suffer immediately by experiencing turbulent thoughts and emotions, but also, again regardless of whether we believe in karma or not, the actions we create tend to be negative, destructive and non-virtuous. Therefore, the more we cultivate altruism and a sense of caring, the greater will be the benefit that we ourselves enjoy.

Neither is this phenomenon confined to the human realm; affection and a sense of caring also play a role in the animal kingdom. Animals that are cruel and aggressive seem to get ostracized from the social group while those that are more accommodating and gentle tend to be much more accepted.

Even within cyclic existence, much of our happiness and satisfaction actually derives from altruism and sense of caring. These qualities offer us unlimited benefit, even in everyday life. Therefore, we should share the sentiments expressed by Shantideva in his *Guide to the Bodhisattva's Way of Life,* where he stated that we should wish to be of service to and utilized by all other sentient beings, just as are the earth, mountains and trees. When we think about altruism in such depth, we will realize that independent self-interest, the interests of the individual I, are totally meaningless, and will truly understand what Shantideva meant in that beautiful verse towards the end of his *Guide,* which I quoted before but will mention again:

For as long as space exists,
For as long as sentient beings remain,
Until then, may I too remain
And dispel the miseries of the world.

When you dedicate your entire being, your body, speech and mind, to fulfilling the single goal of being of benefit to others, you can say that true happiness has begun and you have entered the path to full enlightenment.

You will also appreciate the sentiments expressed by Atisha Dipamkara, when he said that you should not become discouraged even if you spend eons pursuing the practice of the two bodhicittas—the conventional bodhicitta of the altruistic intention and the ultimate bodhicitta of the realization of emptiness. His point was that no matter how long it takes you to develop bodhicitta, once you have single-pointedly dedicated yourself to this goal, you will never harbor the thought that you are wasting your time in any part of your mind. Bodhicitta is the sole pursuit in which you should engage. As Atisha said, "What else can you do in your quest for enlightenment other than practice bodhicitta?" Therefore, regardless of how long it takes, any time spent trying to develop bodhicitta is time spent in the most meaningful way.

When you are happy and things are going well, you should practice bodhicitta, because it will protect you from becoming inflated with ego and from disparaging or insulting others. When you are suffering and facing adversity or misfortune, you should also practice bodhicitta, because it will protect you from losing hope and feeling depressed. As long as you are alive, you should practice bodhicitta, because it will make your existence meaningful and full of purpose. Even when you are dying, you should still practice bodhicitta, because it is the one thing that will never deceive you or let you down.

Having contemplated how, on the basis of his own experience, the

Buddha taught this ideal of bodhicitta, how it contains the entire essence of all his teachings and how fortunate you are to have been introduced to this great principle, you should cultivate the thought, "I shall now dedicate myself exclusively to the practice of bodhicitta. For me, as a practitioner, this is the sole task that lies ahead." Generate within yourself a deep sense of joy and fulfillment mixed with sadness towards the suffering of other sentient beings. Along with all these emotions, generate the strong determination, "I shall never abandon this altruistic intention." It is with such thoughts that you should participate in the ceremony for affirming the generation of the mind of enlightenment.

8

THE CEREMONY FOR GENERATING BODHICITTA

INTRODUCTION

T O PARTICIPATE IN THE CEREMONY for affirming and enhancing your generation of the altruistic intention, first visualize that Shakyamuni Buddha is here in person, surrounded by such disciples as Maitreya, Manjushri, Nagarjuna, Arya Asanga and the other great Indian masters of the past, whose writings we continue to enjoy and derive benefit from to this day and which serve to open our eye of awareness. Reflect upon the kindness of these masters, as well as that of the Buddha and the bodhisattvas. Also imagine the presence of the great masters from all four traditions of Tibetan Buddhism—Nyingma, Sakya, Kagyü and Geluk—going back to when Buddhism first started to flourish in Tibet in the seventh to eighth centuries. Practitioners from other Buddhist traditions should visualize the lineage masters and historical teachers of their own traditions in the assembly.

Most importantly, visualize that you are surrounded by all other sentient beings. If this is difficult, simply reflect upon the fundamental equality of yourself and all other sentient beings insofar as the natural desire to seek happiness and overcome suffering is concerned. Just as you have the right and natural potential to fulfill this basic aspiration to be happy and overcome suffering, so too do all the other infinite sentient beings.

Then reflect on the fact that when you think of your own self-interest, regardless of your level of importance, you are simply thinking about the concerns of a single individual, but when you think of the interests of others, you are thinking about the welfare of an infinite number of beings. To sacrifice the welfare of countless others for the benefit of one, therefore, is not only foolish but also immoral. Furthermore, it is impractical, because it is a deluded way of trying to fulfill your own aspirations.

Next contemplate the idea that you have held this self-centeredness and self-cherishing attitude at the core of your being since beginningless time, continually trying to fulfill your basic aspirations to be happy and overcome suffering from a self-centered perspective. But if you look at the situation you're in today, you'll see that actually, you haven't made any progress, even after this infinite number of lifetimes. If self-centeredness really had the potential to bring you the benefits you seek, it should have done so by now.

Conclude, therefore, that under the control of self-cherishing since beginningless time, you have made one mistake after another, and now, it's enough. Generate the strong determination never to travel this deluded path again. Compare yourself with great beings such as the Buddha and the bodhisattvas on the path to enlightenment and realize that all their achievements have come from working for others instead of for themselves. Make this firm resolution: "As a Dharma practitioner, from now on, I must work for the benefit of all sentient beings. I will attain buddhahood for their sake, to liberate them from suffering and lead them to enlightenment," and with that, participate in the ceremony for generating bodhicitta.

THE SEVEN-LIMB PRACTICE

In the eighth verse of A Lamp for the Path, Atisha recommends that the bodhicitta ceremony be preceded by the seven-limb puja. If you are participating in this ceremony in order to generate bodhicitta, don't simply listen to my explanations as a lecture, but fold your hands to your heart and pay attention with deep faith in the buddhas and bodhisattvas. Otherwise, you can just listen as normal.

Homage

The first of the seven limbs is the paying of homage. Reflect upon the qualities of Buddha, Dharma and Sangha, particularly the qualities of the Buddha's enlightened body, speech and mind, such as his omniscient mind, his perfection of the altruistic aspiration and his perfection of the wisdom realizing emptiness. Then cultivate the aspiration to gain the wisdom of the Buddha yourself, and with reverence born from deep admiration and respect for the qualities upon which you have reflected, pay homage to the Buddha.

Offering

The second limb is that of making offerings. Imagine offering whatever you own, such as your body and resources, to all the buddhas and bodhisattvas. You can also offer mentally everything else that exists in the universe. Most importantly, however, you should offer all your past virtuous actions of body, speech and mind. You can imagine these positive activities in the form of various articles of offering or you can reflect upon your entire collection of merit and, from the depths of your heart, offer it up to all the buddhas and bodhisattvas.

Confessing

The third limb is the practice of confession, or purification. Reflect upon all the negativities you have ever created through body, speech and mind and how they are all causes for future suffering. Each and every one of us confronts both physical and psychological problems and difficulties; we are beset with sufferings without end, like ripples on a lake, one after the other.

As you think about this, understand that suffering does not arise without reason; every problem has its own cause, the root cause being your own negative actions of body, speech and mind. Imagining that you are in the presence of the noble assembly of buddhas and bodhisattvas, fully disclose all your negative actions and, cultivating a heartfelt sense of regret for them, commit yourself to purifying them.

Rejoicing

Next is the limb of rejoicing. Reflect upon the wonderful enlightened qualities of the buddhas, particularly those of the historical Buddha. We all know that Shakyamuni Buddha was not a fully enlightened being right from the start. Initially, he was just like us—an ordinary being struggling on the path, with the natural weaknesses and limitations that we all have. What distinguishes the Buddha from us, however, is that he took the practice of bodhicitta to heart. He then embarked upon the path and, as a result of his efforts, eventually attained the fully enlightened state.

Therefore, in this practice, rejoice in the Buddha's enlightened qualities and the entire path to enlightenment. Then focus your attention on the bodhisattvas on the last three of the ten bodhisattva grounds [Skt: *bhumi*], who have totally overcome their afflictive thoughts and emotions and are on the threshold of buddhahood. Reflecting upon such beings, develop a deep sense of admiration for their realizations and other spiritual attainments.

Then focus your attention on the bodhisattvas on the first seven grounds. Although they have yet to overcome the power of their afflictions, they are still arya bodhisattvas—bodhisattvas who have a realization of emptiness. Reflecting upon their qualities, develop a deep sense of admiration for them. Next, shift your attention to the bodhisattvas on the first two of the five paths, the paths of accumulation and preparation. They are almost at the same level as us, particularly those on the first path. In a sense, the bodhisattvas right at the beginning of the path are even more amazing than those who are more advanced, because despite being under the control of afflictions such as attachment and hostility, they still have the courage to commit themselves to the ideals of bodhicitta.

We should therefore feel the delight that parents do when their child takes its first faltering steps or speaks its first few words. They don't criticize their child's clumsy gait or limited vocabulary but instead are full of wonder. We can view bodhisattvas struggling at the beginning of the path in the same way, as amazing, awe-inspiring beings.

Having developed a deep sense of admiration for all bodhisattvas, next rejoice at the achievements and qualities of the arhats, who have gained complete freedom from samsara. Also feel a deep appreciation for the attainments of practitioners on the path to liberation.

Finally, rejoice at all the virtue accumulated by your fellow sentient beings and reflect particularly upon your own collection of merit. The fact that you have received a human rebirth endowed with the opportunity to practice Dharma is clear evidence that you have created much merit in the past—encountering the precious, sacred teachings of the Buddha and having an interest in practicing them can only be consequences of past virtuous acts. You have also engaged in many positive, altruistic activities in this life, so, recalling all this virtue, dedicate it to the welfare of all sentient beings and rejoice in the opportunities you have had to create all this merit.

Requesting

Fifth is the limb of requesting the buddhas to turn the wheel of Dharma. This practice is associated with the Buddha in his nirmanakaya form. Direct your attention to those newly enlightened buddhas who have not yet started to teach Dharma and beg them to turn the wheel of Dharma in order to fulfill their pledge to work for the benefit of all sentient beings.

Beseeching

The sixth limb is that of appealing to the buddhas not to enter final nirvana. Again, this is mainly directed at buddhas in their nirmanakaya form, who have turned the wheel of Dharma and performed many enlightened deeds. Beg them not to enter final nirvana but to remain serving sentient beings.

Dedication

The seventh and final limb is that of dedication. Dedicate all the merit you have ever accumulated, particularly that of taking the bodhicitta vow, to the well-being of all sentient beings and to the attainment of enlightenment for their benefit.

THE ACTUAL CEREMONY FOR GENERATING BODHICITTA

The actual ceremony for generating the mind of enlightenment can be conducted on the basis of reading the following three verses. The first presents the practice of taking refuge in the Three Jewels; the second is the actual generation of the altruistic intention; the third helps enhance the mind that has been generated, to sustain it without degeneration.

Kneel on one knee, if that is convenient; otherwise, remain seated. While reciting these verses, contemplate their meaning. Remember that as bodhisattva practitioners, when you take refuge in the Three Jewels, you are taking Mahayana refuge, engaging in this practice for the benefit of all sentient beings, and are motivated by the thought of attaining enlightenment for their benefit.

Repeat the following verses three times:

With the wish to free all beings
I shall always go for refuge
To Buddha, Dharma and Sangha.

Until I reach full enlightenment,
Inspired by wisdom and compassion,
Today, in the Buddha's presence,
I generate the mind of full awakening
For the benefit of all sentient beings.

As long as space remains
As long as sentient beings remain
Until then may I too remain
And dispel the miseries of the world.

In this way, generate the altruistic intention of bodhicitta. Although you have not taken a formal pledge, since you have generated bodhicitta here today, it would be helpful to ensure that your practice of bodhicitta does not degenerate. Therefore, it would be very beneficial for you to recite and think about the meaning of these three verses on a daily basis.

9

BODHISATTVA OUTLOOK AND ACTION

Lamp for the Path: Verse 18

> Having developed the aspiration for enlightenment,
> Constantly enhance it through concerted effort.
> To remember it in this and also in other lives,
> Keep the precepts properly as explained.

If you have taken a formal pledge of bodhicitta, you have to abstain from the four negative factors and cultivate the four positive ones to ensure that your practice does not degenerate in this and future lifetimes.

The four negative factors are:

1. Deceiving your teacher and beings worthy of veneration by telling lies.
2. Causing others to feel remorse for their virtuous deeds.
3. Out of anger, speaking harshly to bodhisattvas.
4. With negative motivation, deceiving other sentient beings.

The four positive factors are:

1. Never telling lies for selfish reasons, even at the cost of your life.
2. Leading other beings to the path of virtue.
3. Cultivating recognition of bodhisattvas who have generated bodhicitta as teachers and proclaiming their virtues.
4. Continuously maintaining your compassion and sense of responsibility for all sentient beings.

Lamp for the Path: Verse 19

Without the vow of the engaged intention,
Perfect aspiration will not grow.
Make effort definitely to take it,
Since you want the wish for enlightenment to grow.

Here, the text is stating that although generating the aspiration to attain enlightenment for the sake of all sentient beings has tremendous merit, greater benefit lies in actually taking the bodhisattva vows to live the ideals of bodhicitta. The text suggests the following sequence:

1. Generate the altruistic intention.
2. Participate in a ceremony and take a pledge to continue to sustain it.
3. Cultivate the desire to engage in the bodhisattva deeds.
4. Take the bodhisattva vows.

Lamp for the Path: Verse 20

Those who maintain any of the seven kinds
Of individual liberation vow

Have the ideal [prerequisite] for
The bodhisattva vow, not others.

Here, the text points out that practitioners who take the bodhisattva vows ideally should have laid the foundation of ethical discipline by observing any of the seven classes of the vows for individual liberation:

1. Layman vows.
2. Laywoman vows.
3. Novice monk vows.
4. Novice nun vows.
5. Probationary nun vows.
6. Fully ordained monk vows.
7. Fully ordained nun vows.

Lamp for the Path: Verse 21

The Tathagata spoke of seven kinds
Of individual liberation vow.
The best of these is glorious pure conduct,
Said to be the vow of a fully ordained person.

This verse states that of these seven categories of pratimoksha vows, the highest is that of full ordination. The Buddha stated very clearly that we can determine the viability of his doctrine on the basis of the practice of vinaya, the codes of ethical discipline. Wherever the practice of vinaya is established, particularly its three main activities—the periodical confessional ceremonies [Tib: *so-jong*], the summer retreat [Tib: *yar-nä*], and the ending of the summer retreat Tib: *gak-ye*]—the teachings of the Buddha also exist. It is said that wherever the practice of vinaya flourishes, the Buddha himself feels a sense of humility. Wherever the practice of these activities is absent, the teachings of the Buddha cannot be said to truly exist at that place.

This praise of vinaya practice is not only found in the vinaya literature but also in Mahayana texts, such as the bodhisattva sutras and the
texts of Highest Yoga Tantra. In the Kalachakra tantra, for example,
there is an explicit statement that of all the vajra masters of Kalachakra,
the vajra master who has full ordination vows is supreme.

Lamp for the Path: Verse 22

> According to the ritual described in
> The chapter on discipline in the *Bodhisattva Stages,*
> Take the vow from a good
> And well-qualified spiritual teacher.

Unlike the pratimoksha and tantric vows, you can take the bodhisattva vow in
front of a representation of a buddha without the presence of a teacher. However,
Verse 22 states that ideally, you should still take it from a qualified spiritual
teacher. Verse 23 describes the qualities that such a teacher should possess:

Lamp for the Path: Verse 23

> Understand that a good spiritual teacher
> Is one skilled in the vow ceremony,
> Who lives by the vow and has
> The confidence and compassion to bestow it.

The text then goes on to state that if you do not find such a spiritual
teacher, you can still take the vow in the following way:

Lamp for the Path: Verse 24

> However, in the case you try but cannot

> Find such a spiritual teacher,
> I shall explain another
> Correct procedure for taking the vow.

From Verse 25 onwards, the text presents the procedure for taking the bodhisattva vow if a teacher is not available. This is taken from Shantideva's *Compendium of Deeds.*

Lamp for the Path: Verses 25 through 31

> 25. I shall write here very clearly, as explained
>   In the *Ornament of Manjushri's Buddha Land Sutra,*
>   How, long ago, when Manjushri was Ambaraja,
>   He aroused the intention to become enlightened.

(Verse 26 onwards is taken directly from Shantideva's text.)

> 26. "In the presence of the protectors,
>   I arouse the intention to gain full enlightenment.
>   I invite all beings as my guests
>   And shall free them from cyclic existence.

> 27. "From this moment onwards
>   Until I attain enlightenment,
>   I shall not harbor harmful thoughts,
>   Anger, avarice or envy.

> 28. "I shall cultivate pure conduct,
>   Give up wrong-doing and desire
>   And with joy in the vow of discipline
>   Train myself to follow the buddhas.

29. "I shall not be eager to reach
     Enlightenment in the quickest way,
     But shall stay behind till the very end,
     For the sake of a single being.

30. "I shall purify limitless
     Inconceivable lands
     And remain in the ten directions
     For all those who call my name.

31. "I shall purify all my bodily
     And verbal forms of activity.
     My mental activities, too, I shall purify
     And do nothing that is non-virtuous."

In Verse 32, the text presents the practices or precepts in which practitioners must engage once they have taken the bodhisattva vow. These are primarily the practices of the six perfections—generosity, ethical discipline, patience, joyous effort, meditative concentration and wisdom. All the perfections of the bodhisattva practice can be understood in terms of the three ethical disciplines of the bodhisattva:

1. Refraining from negative actions.
2. Accumulating virtue.
3. Working for the welfare of other sentient beings.

Lamp for the Path: Verse 32

When those observing the vow
Of the active altruistic intention have trained well
In the three forms of discipline, their respect

For these three forms of discipline grows,
Which causes purity of body, speech and mind.

THE PRACTICE OF THE FIRST FIVE PERFECTIONS

Now we refer to Lama Tsong Khapa's text to read the explanations of the six perfections. First is the perfection of generosity.

THE PERFECTION OF GENEROSITY

Lines of Experience: Verse 15

> Generosity is the wish-granting jewel with which you can fulfill the hopes of sentient beings. It is the best weapon for cutting the knot of miserliness. It is the (altruistic) conduct that enhances your self-confidence and undaunted courage. It is the basis for your good reputation to be proclaimed in the ten directions. Knowing this, the wise have devoted themselves to the excellent path of completely giving away their body, belongings and merit. I, the yogi, have practiced just that. You who also seek liberation, please cultivate yourself in the same way.

We have to understand that the main purpose of generosity is to fulfill the wishes of the object of generosity, that is other sentient beings. Its purpose for practitioners is to help them overcome feelings of possessiveness and miserly attachment. The texts contain detailed explanations of how to engage in giving: the appropriateness of timing, motivation, state of mind and so forth. Also, when performing an act of generosity, bodhisattva practitioners must ensure that all six perfections are complete within that single act.

THE PERFECTION OF ETHICAL DISCIPLINE

Lines of Experience: Verse 16

> Ethical discipline is the water that washes away the
> stains of faulty actions. It is the ray of moonlight that
> cools the scorching heat of the defilements. (It makes
> you) radiant like a Mount Meru in the midst of the
> nine kinds of being. By its power, you are able to bend
> all beings (to your good influence) without (recourse
> to) mesmerizing glares. Knowing this, the holy ones
> have safeguarded, as they would their eyes, the precepts
> that they have accepted (to keep) purely. I, the yogi,
> have practiced just that. You who also seek liberation,
> please cultivate yourself in the same way.

This verse refers principally to the practice of ethical discipline in the form of
restraint, that is, refraining from negative actions, particularly in the context of
the vows of individual liberation. For a bodhisattva, the main ethical practice
of restraint is to refrain from self-centeredness and self-cherishing thoughts.

THE PERFECTION OF FORBEARANCE

Lines of Experience: Verse 17

> Patience is the best adornment for those with power
> and the perfect ascetic practice for those tormented by
> delusions. It is the high-soaring eagle as the enemy of
> the snake of anger, and the thickest armor against the
> weapons of abusive language. Knowing this, (the wise)
> have accustomed themselves in various ways and forms

to the armor of supreme patience. I, the yogi, have
practiced just that. You who also seek liberation, please
cultivate yourself in the same way.

The practice of patience here refers mainly to developing the forbearance to endure any harm that may befall you, such that you cultivate a
sense of indifference towards it. You learn to voluntarily accept hard-
ships for a higher cause. There is also a third dimension to the practice
of patience, which is cultivated as a result of constantly reflecting upon
the teachings of the Dharma. The most detailed explanations of these
practices can be found in the sixth chapter of Shantideva's *Guide to the
Bodhisattva's Way of Life.*[38]

THE PERFECTION OF JOYOUS EFFORT

Lines of Experience: Verse 18

> Once you wear the armor of resolute and irreversible
> joyous effort, your expertise in the scriptures and
> insights will increase like the waxing moon. You will
> make all your actions meaningful (for attaining
> enlightenment) and will bring whatever you undertake
> to its intended conclusion. Knowing this, the bod-
> hisattvas have exerted great waves of joyous effort,
> washing away all laziness. I, the yogi, have practiced
> just that. You who also seek liberation, please cultivate
> yourself in the same way.

The practice of cultivating this perfection of joyous effort is detailed in
the seventh chapter of Shantideva's *Guide to the Bodhisattva's Way of Life.*

THE PERFECTION OF CONCENTRATION

Lamp for the Path: Verses 33 through 38

From Verse 33 onwards, the *Lamp* gives a detailed explanation of the practices for cultivating calm abiding and penetrative insight.

> 33. Therefore, through effort in the vow made by
> Bodhisattvas for pure, full enlightenment,
> The collections for complete enlightenment
> Will be thoroughly accomplished.

> 34. All buddhas say the cause for the completion
> Of the collections, whose nature is
> Merit and exalted wisdom,
> Is the development of higher perception.

The merit and exalted wisdom mentioned here refer to the two accumulations of merit and wisdom and relate to the two enlightened holy bodies of rupakaya and dharmakaya respectively. The text states that the basis of the completion of these two accumulations is the cultivation of higher perception [Tib: *ngön-she*]. This refers to a heightened awareness where one has the ability to intuit the mental disposition and inclinations of other sentient beings and can act to help them in the most effective way.

> 35. Just as a bird with undeveloped
> Wings cannot fly in the sky,
> Those without the power of higher perception
> Cannot work for the good of living beings.

The point here is that if you lack this awareness of the minds of other sentient beings, while your intentions may be very noble, you might perform activities of body, speech or mind that finish up harming those on the receiving end.

36. The merit gained in a single day
     By one who possesses higher perception
     Cannot be gained even in a hundred lifetimes
     By one without such higher perception.

37. Those who want swiftly to complete
     The collections for full enlightenment
     Will accomplish higher perception
     Through effort, not through laziness.

38. Without the attainment of calm abiding,
     Higher perception will not occur.
     Therefore make repeated effort
     To accomplish calm abiding.

Atisha presents the practice of calm abiding as a condition for the cultivation of this higher perception, or heightened awareness. More importantly, the attainment of calm abiding is a prerequisite for the attainment of vipashyana—penetrative insight into the nature of emptiness. Although it is possible to develop the wisdom realizing emptiness without calm abiding, it is obviously not possible to develop the wisdom that is a union of calm abiding and penetrative insight. True penetrative insight focused on emptiness comes about only when we experience the physical and mental pliancy derived from a process of analytic inquiry. In order to attain the pliancy derived through analysis, we must have the physical and mental pliancy that is generated through single-pointedness of mind. Lama Tsong Khapa's text goes on to describe the distinctive qualities of mind once one has attained calm abiding.

Lines of Experience: Verse 19

> Meditative concentration is the king wielding power
> over the mind. If you fix it (on one point), it remains
> there, immovable like a mighty Mount Meru. If you
> apply it, it can engage fully with any virtuous object. It
> leads to the great exhilarating bliss of your body and
> mind being made serviceable. Knowing this, yogis who
> are proficient have devoted themselves continuously to
> single-pointed concentration, which overcomes the
> enemy of mental wandering. I, the yogi, have practiced
> just that. You who also seek liberation, please cultivate
> yourself in the same way.

In the first two lines, the author is saying that when you have gained calm
abiding, you have also gained a certain mastery over your own mind, because
you have the ability to determine whether or not to engage with an object. If
you want to place it single-pointedly upon a chosen object, it can remain
there completely immovable, like Mount Meru. The kind of meditative concentration described in this verse is attained after the ninth level of mental stability, where you experience an exhilarating sense of bliss.[39] This bliss should
not be confused with the great bliss in the tantric context; rather, it is a bliss
derived from the physical and mental pliancy generated as a result of fusing
your mind single-pointedly with a chosen object of meditation.

Lamp for the Path: Verses 39 & 40

> 39. While the conditions for calm abiding
>   Are incomplete, meditative stabilization
>   Will not be accomplished, even if one meditates
>   Strenuously for thousands of years.

40. Thus maintaining well the conditions mentioned
    In the *Collection for Meditative Stabilization Chapter,*
    Place the mind on any one
    Virtuous focal object.

As the text states, if the conditions for cultivating single-pointedness of mind and calm abiding are not complete, all your efforts to attain it will be wasted. Therefore, if you want to engage in a concerted practice of cultivating calm abiding, first you must ensure that the following five conditions are present:

1. The sound basis of an ethically disciplined way of life.
2. Few personal needs or mundane chores to be done.
3. A good understanding of all the key elements and stages of the practice.
4. An appropriate diet and avoidance of excessive eating.
5. As few distractions as possible, with restriction of interactions with strangers or other people.

In this way, you can create the conditions necessary for the single-pointed practice of calm abiding. Buddhist practitioners making a concerted effort to cultivate this single-pointedness of mind must engage in this practice in two ways. You should know the techniques for both uplifting your mind and generating sobering thoughts. You might think that sitting up straight will uplift your mind and hunching over will bring it down, but neither is really the case. You have to learn the thought processes and reflections that bring about these effects.

Here, we are talking about lam-rim practitioners who have engaged in the practices up to this point—those of the initial and middling scopes, including the Three Higher Trainings—and gained a certain degree of experience as a result of the combined application of analytic meditation and single-pointed placement.

As to the actual steps involved in engaging in the cultivation of calm abiding, there are various methods explained in texts, such as Maitreya/Asanga's *Madhyantavibhaga* [Tib: *U-tha-nam-che*], where we find discussions of the five primary obstacles to successful meditation and the eight antidotes to these obstacles. Regarding the object that you use for single-pointed meditation, the text presents many different categories of object. There are objects that are suited to the purification of negativity or elimination of afflictions, objects that are more suited to analytic temperaments and so forth. Three principal kinds of object are mentioned:

1. A pervasive object, which is one common to both calm abiding and penetrative insight.
2. Objects associated with your own past habits.
3. Objects that are more relevant to overcoming afflictions.

Whether you take an external physical object as the object of your meditation or an instance of your own personal experience, it is important to choose only one object and not keep changing it. The more new objects that you bring in as a focus of your meditation, the less progress you will make. Select a single object and give it your full attention. Buddhist practitioners, for example, can focus on an image of the Buddha. If you do this, however, it is better not to imagine a Buddha that is too big or too small—one about three or four finger-widths in height is quite useful. Whatever the case, your visualization should be clear and luminous, like a hologram made of light.

When you cultivate single-pointed meditation on the Buddha, although you may use a physical representation, such as a statue or a painting, when you first begin, this is not what you use in your actual meditation. There, you focus on an image that you create in your mind and cultivate your single-pointed concentration on that. There are also methods for cultivating calm abiding on the basis of deity yoga, where you visualize yourself as the deity, or your physiological energies, where you concentrate on your subtle channels, for example. The latter are Vajrayana practices.

The key to the development of calm abiding is mindfulness, which combines introspection and diligence. It is the continuous application of mindfulness that sustains your attention on your chosen object. This is the heart of placement meditation. Previously we saw how, on the basis of the application of mindfulness, we ensure restraint from negative activity. Therefore, even ethical discipline involves the practice of mindfulness.

Also, the first of the thirty-seven aspects of the path to enlightenment are the four foundations of mindfulness—mindfulness of body, feeling, mind and phenomena. In the context of single-pointed concentration, the key is to develop mindfulness to such a degree that we can sustain it without an instant's distraction. When we engage in single-pointed concentration through the cultivation of calm abiding, we have to be aware of the various faults that can interfere with our practice. For example, even if we are capable of sustaining single-pointed mindfulness, our meditation may lack clarity, or there may be clarity without loss of focus on the object, but our mind lacks vitality.

In general, the faults of meditation are distraction and mental dullness. There are two types of distraction. One is total loss of attention, with no continuity of mindfulness of the object. The other is more subtle, and occurs when, even though there is no loss of focus on the object, another thought arises somewhere in the corner of our mind. Distractions are a sign that our mind is too excited and that we need to engage in thought processes to bring it down to a calmer level.

Another way in which we lose mindfulness of the object is when our mind suffers from mental dullness, or laxity. This simply means that we

ragmen mentationore

are unable to focus on the object of meditation. At other times, even though we might be focused on the object, there's a lack of clarity, or vitality. This is subtle dullness, or laxity, and is an indication that our mind is too downcast. Here, we need to engage in reflections that uplift our mind by creating a feeling of joy.

If you find that your mind is too excited and distractions occur as soon as you engage in single-pointed meditation, you should reflect upon the fact that you are still under the control of negative thoughts and emotions; that these afflictions are still active within you. Contemplate the fact that you are still caught in the bondage of cyclic existence and reflect upon impermanence and death. This will have an immediate sobering effect and lessen mental excitement and distractions.

If, on the other hand, you find that your mind is downcast and lacks vitality, you need to uplift it. Here, you can reflect upon the fact that you possess buddha nature—the nucleus of buddhahood—or upon the great value and preciousness of your human existence and the opportunities it affords you. You can also reflect upon the qualities of Buddha, Dharma and Sangha, particularly the enlightened qualities of the Buddha, or the fact that you can attain the cessation of suffering. Positive thoughts such as these will inspire joy and confidence within you and reinforce your courage.

When you begin to cultivate calm abiding and single-pointed concentration, you have to learn how these complex processes unfold. In particular, it is essential that you discover sobering and uplifting techniques that work in your own meditation practice and the level of equilibrium that is right for you, but only through continued personal practice and experience, can you discover what these are. Your age and physical constitution can also make a difference, particularly your state of health.

However, as you continue to practice over a prolonged period of time, you will progress through the nine stages of mental stability. By the time you reach the ninth, you will have attained a high degree of single-pointed concentration, which then leads to the attainment of the bliss that comes from physical and mental pliancy. At that point, you have attained calm abiding and the first of the four levels of concentration.

If on the basis of this calm abiding you continue to progress along the path by reflecting upon the imperfections of the desire realm, you will eventually cultivate higher states of awareness, such as the other three levels of concentration. As you proceed further, you will attain the formless absorptions. At such heightened states of concentration, your mind will be so subtle that you will temporarily be free of many of the manifest aspects of the afflictions.

10

THE PERFECTION OF WISDOM

THE IMPORTANCE OF THE PERFECTION OF WISDOM

Lamp for the Path: Verse 41

> When the practitioner has gained calm abiding,
> Higher perception will also be gained,
> But without practice of the perfection of wisdom,
> The obstructions will not come to an end.

According to Mahayana Buddhism, of all of the Buddha's discourses, the essential teachings are those in the *Perfection of Wisdom Sutras,* which present the two aspects of the path. Their explicit subject matter is the profound view of emptiness; their implicit subject matter, the stages of the path, or levels of realization. In Verse 41, Atisha states that even when you have gained calm abiding, if you lack the perfection of wisdom, you will not be able to eliminate the obstructions.

Lamp for the Path: Verse 42

> Thus, to eliminate all obstructions
> To liberation and omniscience,
> The practitioner should continually cultivate
> The perfection of wisdom with skillful means.

In this verse, the text presents the importance of engaging in a path that is a union of method and wisdom. The following verses explain the meaning of method and wisdom.

Lamp for the Path: Verses 43 through 46

> 43. Wisdom without skillful means
> And skillful means, too, without wisdom
> Are referred to as bondage.
> Therefore do not give up either.

> 44. To eliminate doubts concerning
> What is called wisdom and what skillful means,
> I shall make clear the difference
> Between skillful means and wisdom.

> 45. Apart from the perfection of wisdom,
> All virtuous practices such as
> The perfection of giving are described
> As skillful means by the Victorious Ones.

> 46. Whoever, under the influence of familiarity
> With skillful means, cultivates wisdom
> Will quickly attain enlightenment—
> Not just by meditating on selflessness.

Lines of Experience: Verse 20

> Profound wisdom is the eye with which to behold profound emptiness and the path by which to uproot (fundamental ignorance), the source of cyclic existence.

It is the treasure of genius praised in all the scriptural
pronouncements and is renowned as the supreme lamp
that eliminates the darkness of closed-mindedness.
Knowing this, the wise who have wished for liberation
have advanced themselves along this path with every
effort. I, the yogi, have practiced just that. You who
also seek liberation, please cultivate yourself in the
same way.

The first sentence makes the point that because emptiness is the fundamental nature of reality—ignorance of which is the root of cyclic
existence—the wisdom realizing emptiness is the eye that allows us to
see reality's true nature. It is only by transcending the deluded perspective of ignorance and generating its opposite, the perspective of
emptiness, that we can eliminate it.

The reason why Lama Tsong Khapa goes on to say that the perfection
of wisdom is the treasure of genius praised in all the scriptural pronouncements is because to attain the omniscient wisdom of the Buddha
is the highest of all spiritual aspirations. Every scriptural pronouncement
of the Buddha was aimed either directly or indirectly at the attainment of
this wisdom. Furthermore, the omniscient wisdom of the Buddha is the
highest perfection of the wisdom of emptiness. Therefore, the *Perfection
of Wisdom Sutras*, the Buddha's teachings on emptiness, can be said to
contain the innermost essence of all his teachings.

Lama Tsong Khapa also describes the wisdom realizing emptiness as
a lamp dispelling the darkness of ignorance. According to Nagarjuna
and other masters, ignorance here must be identified as the fundamental misperception of reality—the grasping at the independent existence
of things and events. The word "wise" is also significant. Although all
followers of the Buddha aspire to liberation, from the Madhyamaka
point of view, the Vaibhashika and Sautrantika practitioners have an

incomplete understanding of the causation of cyclic existence and the nature of enlightenment. In this sense, they are not wise.

THE NATURE OF WISDOM

Lamp for the Path: Verse 47

> Understanding emptiness of inherent existence
> Through realizing that the aggregates, constituents
> And sources are not produced [do not come into being]
> Is described as wisdom.

This reference to the emptiness of inherent existence of all things refers to the ultimate nature of reality. In our ordinary perception of the world, we tend to perceive things as enjoying some kind of absolute status, as having concrete, objective reality. If we subject them to deeper analysis, however, we find that things do not exist in the way that they appear to us. All things and events lack inherent nature, and this absence of inherent nature is their ultimate reality, or emptiness.

Given that things lack inherent existence, their properties, such as coming into being, abiding and ceasing, also lack inherent existence.

EMPTINESS ACCORDING TO DIFFERENT BUDDHIST SCHOOLS

When we talk about no-self, or emptiness, we are talking about something that is to be negated, or denied, and the critical point here is to identify exactly what it is that we are negating. Among the Buddhist schools that accept the teachings on the selflessness of phenomena in addition to the selflessness of persons, the principal ones are the Cittamatra and the Madhyamaka; the explanation of selflessness here is from the perspective of the Madhyamaka. This perspective is clearly explained in Aryadeva's *Four Hundred Verses on the Middle Way*, where he interprets the self that is to be negated in terms of the concept of independence, saying that

> Anything that comes into being dependently
> Lacks independent status.
> This absence of independence is emptiness.
> Therefore, the status of independence
> Is the self that is to be negated.[40]

Of the Mahayana schools that accept the notion of no-self of person and the no-self of phenomena, all schools apart from the Madhyamaka Prasangika, including the Madhyamaka Svatantrika and Cittamatra schools, accept some notion of an intrinsic nature. The Svatantrikas and the Cittamatrins make a subtle distinction between the no-self of person and the no-self of phenomena, maintaining that the no-self of persons is grosser, or coarser, than the no-self of phenomena. From their point of view, what is to be negated in the context of a person is different from what is to be negated in the context of the person's aggregates, or factors of existence.

In Madhyamaka Prasangika writings, however, such as the works of Aryadeva and the texts we are discussing, there is no difference in subtlety between the no-self of persons and the no-self of phenomena. The only distinction between the no-self of persons and the no-self of phenomena is the *bases* upon which selflessness is presented; the teachings on no-self are presented in relation to either persons or phenomena, such as the aggregates.

There are certain groups of Madhyamaka thinkers who accept some notion of intrinsic nature, albeit at the conventional level, but there's another group of Madhyamaka scholars who totally reject the notion of inherent existence anywhere, even at the conventional level. How did this fundamental divide come into being? The foundational texts of Middle Way thought are Nagarjuna's *Fundamentals of the Middle Way* and Aryadeva's *Four Hundred.* Two distinct interpretations evolved from these texts. Buddhapalita, for example, wrote a commentary on Nagarjuna's *Fundamentals* and developed a line of interpretation rejecting any notion of intrinsic existence, even at the conventional level.

Later, Bhavaviveka wrote his own commentary, *The Lamp of Wisdom (Prajnapradipa),* in which he took issue with Buddhapalita. He also wrote other texts, such as the *Heart of the Middle Way* and its commentary, *Blaze of Reasoning,* which I mentioned before, when talking about the lineage of the Kadampa teachings (see p. 36). These two texts refuting the ideas of the Cittamatra School clearly reveal that the author himself subscribed to some notion of intrinsic existence, at least on the conventional level.

Bhavaviveka then notes that it is our consciousness that is the real, defined person and the referent of our personal terms. Again, this indicates that he accepts some notion of inherent existence. Also, when disputing Buddhapalita, Bhavaviveka presents an epistemology in his commentary on Nagarjuna's *Fundamentals* in which it is evident that he accepts some notion of the intrinsic nature of objects.[41]

If you want to deepen your understanding of emptiness, it is very helpful to look at how the different Buddhist philosophical schools understand no-self.[42] To summarize, Vaibhashikas and Sautrantikas understand emptiness as self and person devoid of substantial reality. Cittamatrins, in addition to accepting the no-self of person, also accept the no-self of phenomena. They interpret the no-self of phenomena as the absence of duality between subject and object, and also through the notion that the referents of terms and concepts do not exist in some absolute, intrinsic manner. Madhyamaka Svatantrikas follow Nagarjuna's teachings but present their own interpretation of emptiness, accepting a degree of intrinsic existence at the conventional level.

If you subject these positions to deeper analysis and reasoning, however, all these ideas, particularly those of the Madhyamaka Svatantrikas, can be shown to be untenable because they take for granted some notion of inherent existence. They also posit a faculty of experience known as reflexive, or self-cognizing, awareness, and it is on the basis of this awareness that they explain the inherent existence of consciousness.

The fact remains, however, that all Madhyamaka thinkers, Prasangikas and Svatantrikas alike, are united in rejecting any notion of true, or ultimate, existence across the entire spectrum of reality. In this respect, they differ from the Cittamatra School, where a distinction is made between the external reality of matter and the internal reality of subjective experience. Cittamatrins reject the true existence of the external material world but maintain the true existence of internal consciousness. Madhyamikas, on the other hand, reject any notion of true existence right across the board.

However, there are two camps within Madhyamaka thought. One rejects the notion of inherent existence even on the conventional level; the other accepts the notion of inherent existence on the conventional level. The question then arises, which of these two distinct readings of Nagarjuna's and Aryadeva's texts should we follow? As is generally the case in Buddhist teachings, we have to subject these ideas to critical analysis and relate them to our own personal experience. When we do this, such notions as the inherent existence of our faculty of perception and self-cognizing awareness all turn out to be untenable because they are refuted by critical reasoning. In general, Buddhist procedure is that any system of thought that is subject to fewer critical objections is more acceptable than one that contains more contradiction and inconsistency.

When you reflect upon the teachings on no-self—particularly upon the significance of presenting the teachings on no-self in relation to person and its factors of existence—you will appreciate the following fundamental point. Although there is a wide spectrum of reality, it is the individual and phenomena that relate to his or her experience of pain and pleasure, happiness and suffering—such as the individual's own mind-body aggregates—that are of immediate relevance. Therefore, right from the beginning, we make a distinction between the person and the person's objects of experience.

When we relate this teaching to our own personal experience, however, we can observe that when the thought, "I am," arises in us, it does so on the basis of our physical or mental constituents; our aggregates underlie "I am." We grasp at these aggregates, and it is on the basis of this grasping and the thought "I am" that we identify with them. This is how the grasping at phenomena serves as the basis for the grasping at the self of the person.

DEPENDENT ORIGINATION

Grasping at phenomena obviously relates to the question of emptiness. When we reflect upon the meaning of emptiness, it is helpful to refer to Nagarjuna's *Fundamentals of the Middle Way*, where he entertains many objections from those who criticize his central conclusion that no thing or event possesses inherent existence. His critics object that saying nothing possesses inherent nature is a descent into nihilism, because it rejects the existence of anything. Nagarjuna responds by saying that this objection is based upon a misunderstanding of what he means by emptiness. To paraphrase Nagarjuna, "If you just reflect on the fact that the premise upon which I argue for emptiness is dependent origination, that alone reveals that by emptiness I do not mean nothingness. Emptiness is not to be equated with mere nothingness; it is simply the absence of inherent, independent existence."

Nagarjuna then presents a verse in which he states,

> Whatever is dependently originated,
> I call that to be empty.
> And that too is dependently designated,
> And this is the Middle Way.

What he is saying is that you arrive at the highest meaning of emptiness through dependent origination. When you understand dependent origination, you can reject any notion of independent existence—existence not dependent upon other factors. Things and events are dependently designated because their identity is derived in dependence upon other factors. When you reflect upon emptiness in terms of dependent origination, you can avoid the extremes of both nihilism—that nothing at all exists—and absolutism—that things possess independent existence. This is the meaning of the Middle Way.

Having stated in the *Precious Garland* that a person is not the earth, water, fire or wind elements, the aggregates and so forth, Nagarjuna does not conclude that the person does not exist. Rather, he says, the person is the accumulation of his or her aggregates. This implies that the process by which you cease to identify yourself with your constituent parts leads to an appreciation of the nature of your existence in terms of the dependent origination of its basis.

When you reflect in this way, you come to realize that what you normally feel and believe is actually contrary to the way in which things actually exist. When you think about your own self, you normally feel as if there is something that you can actually pinpoint and to which the term "person" refers. When you examine this in greater detail, however, you discover that there is actually no such unitary entity to which the term "person" refers and that this term is actually contingent upon the aggregation of many factors. When you arrive at this conclusion you realize that the person that you initially believed to exist inherently is actually devoid of inherent existence. This is the meaning of emptiness.

I personally feel that this way of approaching emptiness is more effective than going through an eliminative process of the person being neither body nor perceptions, neither mental formations…and so forth. Once you arrive at the point where, after going through this kind of eliminative process, you realize that the person cannot be found, it is still open to question whether or not you have actually understood emptiness. However, if you approach emptiness through the meaning of dependent origination, your path to the conclusion will be much more successful.

Establishing emptiness through reasoning

Lamp for the Path: Verses 48 through 50

> 48. Something existent cannot be produced
>   Nor something non-existent, like a sky flower.
>   These errors are both absurd and thus
>   Both of the two will not occur either.

> 49. A thing is not produced from itself,
>   Nor from another, also not from both,
>   Nor causelessly either, thus it does not
>   Exist inherently by way of its own entity.

> 50. Moreover, when all phenomena are examined
>   As to whether they are one or many,
>   They are seen not to exist by way of their own entity,
>   And thus are ascertained as not inherently existent.

Verse 48 presents the reasoning behind establishing emptiness by reflecting upon phenomena from the point of view of their results and echoes a verse from Nagarjuna's *Seventy Stanzas on Emptiness,*[43] where he explains that if one posits the intrinsic existence of all things, then the whole idea of things coming into being becomes absurd. Inherent existence implies some kind of independent, objective reality. If things were independent and objective, they would neither come into being nor cease to be.

In Verse 49, emptiness is presented from the point of view of analyzing a thing's causes, while Verse 50 is written from the point of view of the actual entity itself, where the main reasoning is the absence of identity and difference. This refers to the type of reasoning where we take into account the labels of phenomena, such as "self" or "person."

We realize that such terms are designated upon certain bases. In the case of self or person, the designation is the self and its basis is the aggregates of mind and body. There is, therefore, a relationship between self or person and its basis. The reasoning of absence of singularity or plurality suggests that if we examine the relationship between self and the mind-body aggregates and analyze whether self is identical to or independent from them, we will come to the conclusion that the self is neither the same nor different.

We often postulate the inherent existence of things and events on the basis of their effects. We feel that because things can produce effects they must have some inherent objective quality, or property. Also, because things come into being from certain causes and conditions, we think that they must have some intrinsic nature that causes them to occur. Therefore, we often posit the notion of inherent existence, or objective reality, on the basis of causes and effects. This is why, when negating the inherent existence of a phenomenon, we have to approach it from both its effects and its causes, along with the analysis of the nature of existence itself.

Verse 49 presents the "diamond slivers reasoning."[44] When we say that such-and-such a thing originates, if we simply mean that a thing comes into being from its causes, this is acceptable. If, however, we are not satisfied by this mere nominal reality of the concept of origination, we may ask exactly how does something come into being? Is the effect identical with the cause or is the effect distinct from the cause, or did the effect come into being from a cause that is both identical and distinct, or from a cause that is neither identical nor distinct? The moment we ask such questions, we are already searching for some kind of inherent reality of phenomena, at least from the point of view of origination.

If the notion of origination were tenable, it would, of course, imply an inherent, or intrinsic, origination. However, through reasoning we find that a thing does not come from a cause that is either identical to or independent from its effects. Things also do not come from both the causes and effects, nor do they come from neither causes nor effects. We therefore conclude that things do not possess the characteristics of inherent, or intrinsically real, origination. One of the things that we can conclude as a result of this analysis is that those who accept the notion of inherent existence—at least on the conventional level of reality—are forced to also accept that things do come from inherently distinct causes and conditions.

This is clear from Nagarjuna's writings. In the first chapter of *Fundamentals of the Middle Way*, when he rejects the idea of other-production, he states that for those who posit the notion of inherent existence, much of the conventional use of language describing the relationship between an agent and its activity and things and their properties becomes untenable.

For example, when we say that a sprout comes into being or originates from its causes, we are saying that the origination of the sprout is, in a sense, a property or characteristic of the sprout. During the stage of the seed, however, the sprout is yet to be, but we can still say that because the seed is in the process of maturation, the seed is producing the sprout or the sprout is originating. At this point, the activity of origination is there, but the agent (the sprout) does not exist. Nagarjuna states that this is not a problem for those who reject any notion of inherent existence, because they posit concepts such as the seed producing the sprout purely at the level of linguistic transaction. If you posit these concepts by searching for an objective reality, however, then this relationship between a sprout and its origination becomes untenable. It is through this kind of analysis that the notion of the inherent existence of things is rejected from the point of view of their causes and their effects.

At the heart of the Buddha's teachings lie the four seals, or axioms, of Buddhism, and when we summarize the essence of everything the Buddha taught, we find that the basic framework is presented in the context of these four:

1. All composite phenomena are impermanent.
2. All contaminated phenomena are unsatisfactory, or in the nature of suffering.
3. All things and events are empty, or devoid of self-existence.
4. Nirvana is true peace.

It is the third of these—that all phenomena are empty, or devoid of self-existence—on which the *Perfection of Wisdom Sutras* elaborate. In the *Heart Sutra*, the Buddha enumerated the five aggregates and said that each is devoid of self, or inherent, existence. In summarizing this teaching, he states that "form is emptiness, emptiness is form." In other words, there is no emptiness apart from form and there is no form apart from emptiness.[45]

Therefore, when we search for the inherent nature of everything that we experience and perceive, including our five aggregates and all phenomena relevant to our personal experiences of suffering and happiness, we will be unable to find it. The inherent nature of form or any other phenomenon cannot be found. This is why Buddha stated that form is emptiness. However, this does not mean that all phenomena are non-existent. It simply means that all phenomena are devoid of inherent existence. The existence of phenomena can be understood only in terms of their dependent nature. Therefore, Buddha stated that emptiness is form.

There is a very close relationship between form and its emptiness, because they are two aspects of one and the same phenomenon. According to the teaching on the two truths, each and every phenomenon possesses two natures, one at the conventional level of reality and one at the ultimate level. The conventional truth is the reality that can be accepted at the relative level; emptiness is the ultimate truth of all things and events. We must understand that the two truths are not independent of one another but are two different perspectives, or two natures, of the one phenomenon.

When we proceed with our analysis, one thing that helps us understand emptiness is the law of contradictions. In the world, we find factors that naturally contradict and oppose one other. Furthermore, there are certain phenomena that not only contradict one another but are also mutually exclusive—dependence and independence, for example. Something is either dependent or independent; there is no third possibility. Nagarjuna brings this into focus in his *Refutation of Objections (Vigrahavyavartani)*, where he states that if the absence of inherent existence is reversed, existence of inherent existence is automatically established. Things and events are either inherently existent or empty of inherent existence.

When you think like this, you will realize that when you subject all phenomena to reductive analysis and search for their true essence, you will arrive at a point where you cannot find a solid, concrete reality. However, our own personal experience affirms the reality of things, because we experience their effects. Some things cause us pain, others cause us happiness, so they must exist in some way. At the same time, however, these things and events do not possess the inherent, independent existence that we tend to project onto them.

This suggests, as Nagarjuna points out in his *Precious Garland,* that self or person is the aggregation of the six elements of earth, water, fire, wind, space and consciousness. Similarly, the way in which all phenomena exist can be understood only in terms of the aggregation of various factors; they lack any identity that is independent of other factors. As Buddhapalita stated in his commentary on Nagarjuna's *Fundamentals,* if things and events have an inherent intrinsic identity, we should be able to point at something and say, "'That's it." But such is not the case. When we use terms, labels and concepts, we have to apply them on the basis of the aggregation of many factors. This in itself suggests that things and events do not possess inherent or independent reality. Therefore, when you approach emptiness from the perspective of the dependent origination of things, the fact that things are devoid of inherent existence is brought into much sharper relief.

When you study the various presentations of the Buddha's teachings on no-self, including the premises upon which the Buddhist masters interpret them and the reasoning they use to establish their particular understanding, you will gradually come to appreciate the uniqueness of the teachings of the Madhyamaka Prasangika School. Masters such as Buddhapalita and Chandrakirti interpreted Nagarjuna's teachings on emptiness in a unique and excellent way. When you subject their interpretations to critical analysis, you find that their particular reading of Nagarjuna's teachings on emptiness is the one that is the most compatible with valid reasoning and personal experience. If you base your study of emptiness on the writings of these great, authentic teachers, you will greatly deepen your appreciation of the incredible depth and clarity of their teachings.

MEDITATION ON EMPTINESS

When you actually come to meditate on emptiness, it is more effective to meditate on the emptiness of self, or person, before meditating on the emptiness of phenomena. First you should investigate the self in which you believe, at which you grasp. Where does it reside? Is there a self above and beyond the way you experience it? Is there a self beyond the level of appearance? When you subject the inherent existence of your own self to critical analysis and search for its true nature, you will come to realize that it cannot be found. You cannot find a concrete self.

At this point you may ask yourself, does this mean that the self does not exist at all? But that cannot be the correct conclusion, because you know from personal experience that the self does things, is affected by the environment and so forth, all of which suggests that it possesses a certain degree of existence. However, this existence of the self can be understood only in terms of its dependent nature, that is, as a dependently originated phenomenon.

Once you realize this, you can use your understanding of the dependent origination of the self as a premise to reflect upon its emptiness—that although the self exists, it does not possess inherent, intrinsic reality. This is how to use your understanding of dependent origination to arrive at an understanding of emptiness.

How do we determine that something is existent but something else is not? If we take the example of a real person and a dream person, we can see that they are equal in the fact that both of them lack inherent existence and objective reality. However, if we believe that the dream person is real, we can invalidate that belief by other conventional knowledge, such as past experience or third person testimony. Belief in the real person as real cannot be invalidated by such conventional means. This is one method for distinguishing between something that is existent and something that is not.

A second method is to rely upon reasoning based on the ultimate nature of reality. For example, with certain concepts postulated through metaphysical thought processes or by adherents to some metaphysical schools that may not be susceptible to invalidation by conventional knowledge.

When you think along these lines, you appreciate Lama Tsong Khapa's sentiments when, near the end of the emptiness section of his *Great Exposition*, he said, "O, my colleagues, learned in the great Middle Way treatises. Although in your mind it is very difficult to posit notions of cause and effect in a world devoid of inherent existence, nevertheless, embrace and uphold this by hailing it to be the way of the Middle Path."

This suggests that when you deepen your understanding of emptiness, you arrive at a point where the reality of things tends to disappear. Things seem to disintegrate and become insubstantial. This, however, is not an indication that they do not exist but rather that they are devoid of objective, substantial reality. In this instance, although it may be difficult to conceptually maintain the notion of cause and effect and the conventional reality of phenomena, you must persist and continually familiarize yourself with this kind of understanding.

Then, gradually, by constantly relating back to your personal experience, you will become more attuned to the experience of emptiness; more and more comfortable, conceptually and emotionally, with the notion that things and events do not possess inherent existence. This conclusion does not appear in your mind like a flash of lightning; an understanding of emptiness dawns only as the result of a prolonged process of continual reflection.

Lamp for the Path: Verses 51 through 54

> 51. The reasoning of the *Seventy Stanzas on Emptiness*
> The *Treatise on the Middle Way* and so forth

Explain that the nature of all things
Is established as emptiness.

52. Since there are a great many passages,
I have not cited them here,
But have explained just their conclusions
For the purpose of meditation.

53. Thus, whatever is meditation
On selflessness, in that it does not observe
An inherent nature in phenomena,
Is the cultivation of wisdom.

THE NON-CONCEPTUAL UNDERSTANDING OF EMPTINESS

54. Just as wisdom does not see
An inherent nature in phenomena,
Having analyzed wisdom itself by reasoning
Non-conceptually meditate on that.

The reference to non-conceptuality in Verse 54 indicates the stages through which we progress and enhance our realization of emptiness. Through treading the various stages of the path, such as the path of accumulation, and particularly the four levels of the path of preparation,[46] we eventually arrive at an understanding of emptiness that is direct, intuitive and non-conceptual.

The importance of meditating on emptiness is universal among the four schools of Tibetan Buddhism. In the Nyingma School, the practice of *dzog-chen* (particularly the "breakthrough" and "leap-over" practices) includes a preliminary process that is described as searching for the origin, the abiding and the dissolution of the nature of the mind. The meditation on emptiness comes into the picture in the context of this search.

Similarly, the Kagyü teachings on *mahamudra* speak of "single-pointedness," "transcendence of conceptual elaborations," "single taste" and "beyond meditation." In this context, single-pointedness refers to the cultivation of calm abiding, whereas the first part of cultivating transcendence of conceptual elaboration is really the meditation on emptiness.

The Sakya teaching on *sel-tong sung-jug* refers to non-duality and the union of profundity and clarity—profundity refers to the teachings on emptiness; clarity refers to the nature of mind.[47]

In the Geluk, we need to cultivate the wisdom of emptiness in conjunction with the experience of bliss in the context of the practice of cultivating the wisdom that is the indivisible union of bliss and emptiness. In all four schools, the emptiness that is taught is that which Nagarjuna presented in his *Fundamentals of the Middle Way*. Nagarjuna's presentation of emptiness is common to both Paramitayana and Vajrayana. In Vajrayana, however, a unique practice places specific emphasis on cultivating the *subjective* experience of the wisdom of emptiness; the emptiness that is the *object* is common to both sutra and tantra.

Lamp for the Path: Verses 55 through 59

> 55. The nature of this worldly existence,
>   Which has come from conceptualization,
>   Is conceptuality. Thus the elimination of
>   Conceptuality is the highest state of nirvana.

> 56. The great ignorance of conceptuality
>   Makes us fall into the ocean of cyclic existence.
>   Resting in non-conceptual stabilization,
>   Space-like non-conceptuality manifests clearly.

57. When bodhisattvas non-conceptually contemplate
    This excellent teaching, they will transcend
    Conceptuality, so hard to overcome,
    And eventually reach the non-conceptual state.

58. Having ascertained through scripture
    And through reasoning that phenomena
    Are not produced nor inherently existent,
    Meditate without conceptuality.

59. Having thus meditated on suchness,
    Eventually, after reaching "heat" and so forth,
    The "very joyful" and the others are attained
    And, before long, the enlightened state of buddhhood.

THE UNION OF CALM ABIDING AND PENETRATIVE INSIGHT

Lines of Experience: Verse 21

In (a state of) merely single-pointed meditative concentration, you do not have the insight (that gives you)
the ability to cut the root of cyclic existence. Moreover,
devoid of a path of calm abiding, wisdom (by itself) cannot turn back the delusions, no matter how much you
analyze them. Therefore, on the horse of unwavering
calm abiding, (masters) have mounted the discriminating wisdom that is totally decisive about how things exist
[or, the wisdom penetrating the depths of the ultimate
mode of being]. Then, with the sharp weapon of
Middle Path reasoning, devoid of extremes, they have

used wide-ranging discriminating wisdom to analyze
properly and destroy all underlying supports for their
(cognitions) aimed at grasping for extremes. In this
way, they have expanded their intelligence that has
realized emptiness. I, the yogi, have practiced just that.
You who also seek liberation, please cultivate yourself
in the same way.

This verse presents the importance of cultivating the union of calm
abiding and penetrative wisdom focused on emptiness.

Lines of Experience: Verse 22

Once you have achieved single-pointed concentration
through accustoming yourself to single-pointedness of
mind, your examination then of individual phenomena
with the proper analysis should itself enhance your single-minded concentration, settled extremely firmly,
without any wavering, on the actual way in which all
things exist. Seeing this, the zealous have marveled at
the attainment of the union of calm abiding and penetrative insight. Is there need to mention that you should
pray (to attain it as well)? I, the yogi, have practiced just
that. You who also seek liberation, please cultivate yourself in the same way.

This verse points to the possibility of actually reinforcing your single-
pointed stability of mind through a process of analysis. The following
verse presents the difference between the post-meditation session and
the path during the actual meditation session.

Lines of Experience: Verse 23

> (Having achieved such a union) you should meditate
> both on space-like emptiness while completely
> absorbed (in your meditation sessions) and on illusion-
> like emptiness when you subsequently arise. By doing
> this, you will, through your union of method and
> awareness, become praised as someone perfecting the
> bodhisattva's conduct. Realizing this, those with the
> great good fortune (to have attained enlightenment)
> have made it their custom never to be content with
> merely partial paths. I, the yogi, have practiced just
> that. You who also seek liberation, please cultivate
> yourself in the same way.

During the meditation session, you focus primarily on the space-like
nature of reality, which is simply the absence of inherent existence in all
things. When you arise from the session and engage with the world, your
meditation experience should permeate your post-session experience such
that you perceive as illusory everything with which you come into contact.
Although you might perceive objects as having some kind of concrete reality, you realize that in essence, they lack such reality.

We now return to Atisha's *Lamp*. In the context of the Perfection
Vehicle, although the method and wisdom aspects of the path mutually
reinforce and complement one another, they are presented as two distinct continua of consciousness. The profound feature of the Vajrayana
path is that the union of method and wisdom is not a question of two
independent factors complementing one another but rather one of both
factors being present and complete within a single state of mind. This is
achieved through the practice of deity yoga.

THE VAJRAYANA PATH

Lamp for the Path: Verse 60

> If you wish to create with ease
> The collections for enlightenment
> Through activities of pacification,
> Increase and so forth, gained by the power of mantra,

In the next verses, the text goes on to talk about the importance of finding a spiritual teacher and developing a proper reliance on this teacher, and points out that this practice is presented in the context of Vajrayana.

Lamp for the Path: Verses 61 through 67

> 61. And also through the force of the eight
>   And other great attainments like the "good pot"—
>   If you want to practice secret mantra,
>   As explained in the action and performance tantras,
>
> 62. Then, to receive the preceptor initiation,
>   You must please an excellent spiritual teacher
>   Through service, valuable gifts and the like
>   As well as through obedience.
>
> 63. Through the full bestowing of the preceptor initiation,
>   By a spiritual teacher who is pleased,
>   You are purified of all wrong-doing
>   And become fit to gain powerful attainments.

64. Because the *Great Tantra of the Primordial Buddha*
    Forbids it emphatically,
    Those observing pure conduct should not
    Take the secret and wisdom initiations.

65. If those observing the austere practice of pure conduct
    Were to hold these initiations,
    Their vow of austerity would be impaired
    Through doing that which is proscribed.

66. This creates transgressions that are a defeat
    For those observing discipline.
    Since they are certain to fall to a bad rebirth,
    They will never gain accomplishments.

67. There is no fault if one who has received
    The preceptor initiation and has knowledge
    Of suchness listens to or explains the tantras
    And performs burnt offering rituals,
    Or makes offering of gifts and so forth.

Similarly, in Verse 24 of *Lines of Experience*, Lama Tsong Khapa presents
the general procedure of the paths according to Vajrayana.

Lines of Experience: Verse 24

(Renunciation, an enlightened motive and correct view
of emptiness) are necessary in common for (achieving)
supreme paths through either of the two Mahayana
vehicles of (practicing) causes (for enlightenment) or
(simulating now) the results (you will achieve).

Therefore, once you have properly developed like this these (three principal) paths, you should rely on the skillful captain (of a fully qualified tantric master) as your protector, and set out (on this latter, speedier vehicle) across the vast ocean of the (four) classes of tantra. Those who have (done so and) devoted themselves to his or her guideline instructions have made their attainment of (a human body with all) liberties and endowments fully meaningful (by attaining enlightenment in their very lives). I, the yogi, have practiced just that. You who also seek liberation, please cultivate yourself in the same way.

Question and Answer Period

Question. Your Holiness, although my meditation experience is very shallow and weak, when meditating on the lack of inherent existence of self, I become scared at the dawn of that understanding. Is this normal? Is there an antidote?

His Holiness. There are two possibilities. One is that perhaps your understanding of emptiness is not deep enough, in which case there is a danger of your sliding into a nihilistic interpretation of the meaning of emptiness, where emptiness almost becomes a concept of nothingness or non-existence. This can then cause some kind of fear of non-existence. Under such circumstances, it is important to reinforce your conviction in the efficacy of the law of cause and effect, and particularly in the teachings of dependent origination, because the true meaning of emptiness has to be understood in terms of dependent arising. The antidote to this fear is reinforcing your understanding of the dependent origination of things, their cause and effect nature, how they come into being and what kind of conventional, or relative, status they possess.

However, it is also possible that your understanding of emptiness is correct. When you deeply reflect on emptiness, it is not impossible that some kind of fear or anxiety might arise in you, because what we normally take for granted and hold to be unquestionable—this solid, concrete reality and independently existing self—has been shown to be false. This kind of realization can cause a sense of fear, but this fear gradually diminishes as you deepen your understanding of emptiness more and more.

Question. How can the law of dependent origination explain the continuity of mind? Is the mind an independent phenomenon?

His Holiness. It is possible to misunderstand the ever-present continuity of consciousness as being some kind of eternal entity, but just because something retains its continuum does not mean that it is an eternal, unchanging, permanent phenomenon. For example, when we look carefully, we see the tremendous complexity of the world of experience. It is this very complexity, in fact, to which we refer as consciousness, or mind, and it is on the basis of this continuum that we describe states of mind as being of particular types.

Also, we know from our personal experience that our thoughts, emotions and attitudes can change. If the mind were permanent and independent, therefore, there would simply be no room for such changes to occur. The fact that there *is* room for change and transformation suggests that consciousness is a dynamic, ever-changing phenomenon. We can understand consciousness only in terms of a continuum, but this continuum can only be understood in relation to the succession of many events. This already suggests that we are talking about a composite phenomenon and that consciousness is dependently originated.

When we look at things and events, we can see that there is a relationship between the whole and the constituents that come together to compose it. The fact that something is said to be whole immediately suggests its relationship with its constituent parts. The constituent parts are not independent or separate from the whole, nor are they identical to it. There is a relationship between the two.

Question. We have asked Your Holiness many questions. What question would you ask us that we might each answer within ourselves?

His Holiness. Examine yourself to see whether or not you are dedicated to your spiritual practice. This is very important.

DEDICATION

Atisha concludes his *Lamp* with:

> 68. I, the Elder Dipamkarashri, having seen it
> Explained in sutra and in other teachings,
> Have made this concise explanation
> At the request of Jangchub Ö.

And finally, Lama Tsong Khapa makes this dedication:

> 25. In order to accustom this to my own mind and also
> to benefit others as well who have the good fortune
> (to meet a true guru and be able to practice what he
> or she teaches), I have explained here in easily
> understandable words the complete path that pleas-
> es the buddhas. I pray that that the merit from this
> may cause all sentient beings never to be parted
> from these pure and excellent paths. I, the yogi, have
> practiced just that. You who also seek liberation,

please cultivate yourself in the same way.

Then, in the colophon to *Lines of Experience*, we read:

> This concludes the *Abbreviated Points of the Graded Path to Enlightenment*, compiled in brief so that they might not be forgotten. It has been written at Ganden Nampar Gyelwa'i Monastery on Drog Riwoche Mountain, Tibet, by the Buddhist monk Losang Dragpa, a meditator who has heard many teachings.

In conclusion, my wish is that you all try to be warm-hearted people. This is the most important thing. I myself try to be a sincere follower of the Buddha. Even in my dreams, I always remember that I'm a Buddhist monk. This feeling will remain until my death. In the meantime, I try to dedicate my existence to the benefit of others. If you, too, practice in this way, we will truly become genuine, good friends.

APPENDIX 1

A LAMP FOR THE PATH TO ENLIGHTENMENT
by
Atisha Dipamkara Shrijnana
(982–1054)[48]

Homage to the bodhisattva, the youthful Manjushri.

1. I pay homage with great respect
   To the conquerors of the three times,
   To their teaching and to those who aspire to virtue.
   Urged by the good disciple Jangchub Ö
   I shall illuminate the lamp
   For the path to enlightenment.

2. Understand that there are three kinds of persons
   Because of their small, middling and supreme capacities.
   I shall write clearly distinguishing
   Their individual characteristics.

3. Know that those who by whatever means
   Seek for themselves no more
   Than the pleasures of cyclic existence
   Are persons of the least capacity.

4. Those who seek peace for themselves alone,
 Turning away from worldly pleasures
 And avoiding destructive actions
 Are said to be of middling capacity.

5. Those who, through their personal suffering,
 Truly want to end completely
 All the suffering of others
 Are persons of supreme capacity.

6. For those excellent living beings,
 Who desire supreme enlightenment,
 I shall explain the perfect methods
 Taught by the spiritual teachers.

7. Facing paintings, statues and so forth
 Of the completely enlightened one,
 Reliquaries and the excellent teaching,
 Offer flowers, incense—whatever you have.

8. With the seven-part offering
 From the *[Prayer of] Noble Conduct,*
 With the thought never to turn back
 Till you gain ultimate enlightenment,

9. And with strong faith in the Three Jewels,
 Kneeling with one knee on the ground
 And your hands pressed together,
 First of all take refuge three times.

10. Next, beginning with an attitude
    Of love for all living creatures,
    Consider beings, excluding none,
    Suffering in the three bad rebirths,
    Suffering birth, death and so forth.

11. Then, since you want to free these beings
    From the suffering of pain,
    From suffering and the cause of suffering,
    Arouse immutably the resolve
    To attain enlightenment.

12. The qualities of developing
    Such an aspiration are
    Fully explained by Maitreya
    In the *Array of Trunks Sutra*.

13. Having learned about the infinite benefits
    Of the intention to gain full enlightenment
    By reading this sutra or listening to a teacher,
    Arouse it repeatedly to make it steadfast.

14. The *Sutra Requested by Viradatta*
    Fully explains the merit therein.
    At this point, in summary,
    I will cite just three verses.

15. If it possessed physical form,
    The merit of the altruistic intention
    Would completely fill the whole of space
    And exceed even that.

16. If someone were to fill with jewels
    As many buddha fields as there are grains
    Of sand in the Ganges
    To offer to the Protector of the World,

17. This would be surpassed by
    The gift of folding one's hands
    And inclining one's mind to enlightenment,
    For such is limitless.

18. Having developed the aspiration for enlightenment,
    Constantly enhance it through concerted effort.
    To remember it in this and also in other lives,
    Keep the precepts properly as explained.

19. Without the vow of the engaged intention,
    Perfect aspiration will not grow.
    Make effort definitely to take it,
    Since you want the wish for enlightenment to grow.

20. Those who maintain any of the seven kinds
    Of individual liberation vow
    Have the ideal [prerequisite] for
    The bodhisattva vow, not others.

21. The Tathagata spoke of seven kinds
    Of individual liberation vow.
    The best of these is glorious pure conduct,
    Said to be the vow of a fully ordained person.

22. According to the ritual described in
    The chapter on discipline in the Bodhisattva Stages,
    Take the vow from a good
    And well-qualified spiritual teacher.

23. Understand that a good spiritual teacher
    Is one skilled in the vow ceremony,
    Who lives by the vow and has
    The confidence and compassion to bestow it.

24. However, in case you try but cannot
    Find such a spiritual teacher,
    I shall explain another
    Correct procedure for taking the vow.

25. I shall write here very clearly, as explained
    In the *Ornament of Manjushri's Buddha Land Sutra,*
    How, long ago, when Manjushri was Ambaraja,
    He aroused the intention to become enlightened.

26. "In the presence of the protectors,
    I arouse the intention to gain full enlightenment.
    I invite all beings as my guests
    And shall free them from cyclic existence.

27. "From this moment onwards
    Until I attain enlightenment,
    I shall not harbor harmful thoughts,
    Anger, avarice or envy.

28. "I shall cultivate pure conduct,
    Give up wrong-doing and desire
    And with joy in the vow of discipline
    Train myself to follow the buddhas.

29. "I shall not be eager to reach
    Enlightenment in the quickest way,
    But shall stay behind till the very end,
    For the sake of a single being.

30. "I shall purify limitless
    Inconceivable lands
    And remain in the ten directions
    For all those who call my name.

31. "I shall purify all my bodily
    And verbal forms of activity.
    My mental activities, too, I shall purify
    And do nothing that is non-virtuous."

32. When those observing the vow
    Of the active altruistic intention have trained well
    In the three forms of discipline, their respect
    For these three forms of discipline grows,
    Which causes purity of body, speech and mind.

33. Therefore, through effort in the vow made by
    Bodhisattvas for pure, full enlightenment,
    The collections for complete enlightenment
    Will be thoroughly accomplished.

34. All buddhas say the cause for the completion
     Of the collections, whose nature is
     Merit and exalted wisdom,
     Is the development of higher perception.

35. Just as a bird with undeveloped
     Wings cannot fly in the sky,
     Those without the power of higher perception
     Cannot work for the good of living beings.

36. The merit gained in a single day
     By one who possesses higher perception
     Cannot be gained even in a hundred lifetimes
     By one without such higher perception.

37. Those who want swiftly to complete
     The collections for full enlightenment
     Will accomplish higher perception
     Through effort, not through laziness.

38. Without the attainment of calm abiding,
     Higher perception will not occur.
     Therefore make repeated effort
     To accomplish calm abiding.

39. While the conditions for calm abiding
     Are incomplete, meditative stabilization
     Will not be accomplished, even if one meditates
     Strenuously for thousands of years.

40. Thus maintaining well the conditions mentioned
    In the *Collection for Meditative Stabilization Chapter,*
    Place the mind on any one
    Virtuous focal object.

41. When the practitioner has gained calm abiding,
    Higher perception will also be gained,
    But without practice of the perfection of wisdom,
    The obstructions will not come to an end.

42. Thus, to eliminate all obstructions
    To liberation and omniscience,
    The practitioner should continually cultivate
    The perfection of wisdom with skillful means.

43. Wisdom without skillful means
    And skillful means, too, without wisdom
    Are referred to as bondage.
    Therefore do not give up either.

44. To eliminate doubts concerning
    What is called wisdom and what skillful means,
    I shall make clear the difference
    Between skillful means and wisdom.

45. Apart from the perfection of wisdom,
    All virtuous practices such as
    The perfection of giving are described
    As skillful means by the Victorious Ones.

46. Whoever, under the influence of familiarity
    With skillful means, cultivates wisdom

Will quickly attain enlightenment—
Not just by meditating on selflessness.

47. Understanding emptiness of inherent existence
    Through realizing that the aggregates, constituents
    And sources are not produced
    Is described as wisdom.

48. Something existent cannot be produced,
    Nor something non-existent, like a sky flower.
    These errors are both absurd and thus
    Both of the two will not occur either.

49. A thing is not produced from itself,
    Nor from another, also not from both,
    Nor causelessly either, thus it does not
    Exist inherently by way of its own entity.

50. Moreover, when all phenomena are examined
    As to whether they are one or many,
    They are not seen to exist by way of their own entity,
    And thus are ascertained as not inherently existent.

51. The reasoning of the *Seventy Stanzas on Emptiness,*
    The *Treatise on the Middle Way* and so forth
    Explain that the nature of all things
    Is established as emptiness.

52. Since there are a great many passages,
    I have not cited them here,
    But have explained just their conclusions
    For the purpose of meditation.

53. Thus, whatever is meditation
    On selflessness, in that it does not observe
    An inherent nature in phenomena,
    Is the cultivation of wisdom.

54. Just as wisdom does not see
    An inherent nature in phenomena,
    Having analyzed wisdom itself by reasoning,
    Non-conceptually meditate on that.

55. The nature of this worldly existence,
    Which has come from conceptualization,
    Is conceptuality. Thus the elimination of
    Conceptuality is the highest state of nirvana.

56. The great ignorance of conceptuality
    Makes us fall into the ocean of cyclic existence.
    Resting in non-conceptual stabilization,
    Space-like non-conceptuality manifests clearly.

57. When bodhisattvas non-conceptually contemplate
    This excellent teaching, they will transcend
    Conceptuality, so hard to overcome,
    And eventually reach the non-conceptual state.

58. Having ascertained through scripture
    And through reasoning that phenomena
    Are not produced nor inherently existent,
    Meditate without conceptuality.

59. Having thus meditated on suchness,
    Eventually, after reaching "heat" and so forth,

The "very joyful" and the others are attained
And, before long, the enlightened state of buddhahood.

60. If you wish to create with ease
    The collections for enlightenment
    Through activities of pacification,
    Increase and so forth, gained by the power of mantra,

61. And also through the force of the eight
    And other great attainments like the "good pot"—
    If you want to practice secret mantra,
    As explained in the action and performance tantras,

62. Then, to receive the preceptor initiation,
    You must please an excellent spiritual teacher
    Through service, valuable gifts and the like
    As well as through obedience.

63. Through the full bestowing of the preceptor initiation,
    By a spiritual teacher who is pleased,
    You are purified of all wrong-doing
    And become fit to gain powerful attainments.

64. Because the *Great Tantra of the Primordial Buddha*
    Forbids it emphatically,
    Those observing pure conduct should not
    Take the secret and wisdom initiations.

65. If those observing the austere practice of pure conduct
    Were to hold these initiations,
    Their vow of austerity would be impaired
    Through doing that which is proscribed.

66. This creates transgressions that are a defeat
    For those observing discipline.
    Since they are certain to fall to a bad rebirth,
    They will never gain accomplishments.

67. There is no fault if one who has received
    The preceptor initiation and has knowledge
    Of suchness listens to or explains the tantras
    And performs burnt offering rituals,
    Or makes offering of gifts and so forth.

68. I, the Elder Dipamkarashri, having seen it
    Explained in sutra and in other teachings,
    Have made this concise explanation
    At the request of Jangchub Ö.

COLOPHON

This concludes *A Lamp for the Path to Enlightenment*, by the Acharya Dipamkara Shrijnana. It was translated, revised and finalized by the eminent Indian abbot himself and by the great reviser, translator and fully ordained monk Geway Lodrö. This teaching was written in the temple of Thöling in Zhang Zhung. Translated by Ruth Sonam, Dharamsala, January 1997.

Appendix 2

Lines of Experience
by
Lama Je Tsong Khapa (1357–1419)[49]

1. I prostrate before you, (Buddha), head of the Shakya clan. Your enlightened body is born out of tens of millions of positive virtues and perfect accomplishments; your enlightened speech grants the wishes of limitless beings; your enlightened mind sees all knowables as they are.

2. I prostrate before you Maitreya and Manjushri, supreme spiritual children of this peerless teacher. Assuming responsibility (to further) all Buddha's enlightened deeds, you sport emanations to countless worlds.

3. I prostrate before your feet, Nagarjuna and Asanga, ornaments of our Southern Continent. Highly famed throughout the three realms, you have commented on the most difficult to fathom "Mother of the Buddhas" *(Perfection of Wisdom Sutras)* according to exactly what was intended.

4. I bow to Dipamkara (Atisha), holder of a treasure of instructions (as seen in your *Lamp for the Path to Enlightenment*). All the complete, unmistaken points concerning the paths of profound view and vast action, transmitted intact from these two great forerunners, can be included within it.

5. Respectfully, I prostrate before my spiritual masters. You are the eyes allowing us to behold all the infinite scriptural pronouncements, the best ford for those of good fortune to cross to liberation. You make everything clear through your skillful deeds, which are moved by intense loving concern.

6. The stages of the path to enlightenment have been transmitted intact by those who have followed in order both from Nagarjuna and Asanga, those crowning jewels of all erudite masters of our Southern Continent and the banner of whose fame stands out above the masses. As (following these stages) can fulfill every desirable aim of all nine kinds of being, they are a power-granting king of precious instruction. Because they collect the streams of thousands of excellent classics, they are indeed an ocean of illustrious, correct explanation.

7. These teachings make it easy to understand how there is nothing contradictory in all the Buddha's teachings and make every scriptural pronouncement without exception dawn on your mind as a personal instruction. They make it easy to discover what the Buddha intended and protect you as well from the abyss of the great error. Because of these (four benefits), what discriminating person among the erudite masters of India and Tibet would not have his or her mind be completely enraptured by these stages of the path (arranged) according to the three levels of motivation, the supreme instruction to which many fortunate ones have devoted themselves?

8. Although (there is much merit to be gained from) reciting or hearing even once this manner of text (written by Atisha) that includes the essential points of all scriptural pronouncements, you are certain to amass even greater waves of beneficial collections from actually teaching and studying the sacred Dharma (contained therein). Therefore, you should consider the points (for doing this properly).

9. (Having taken refuge,) you should see that the root cause excellent-
ly propitious for as great a mass of good fortune as possible for this
and future lives is proper devotion in thought and action to your
sublime teacher who shows you the path (to enlightenment). Thus
you should please your teacher by offering your practice of exactly
what he or she says, which you would not forsake even at the cost
of your life. I, the yogi, have practiced just that. You who also seek
liberation, please cultivate yourself in the same way.

10. This human existence with its (eight) liberties is much more precious than a wish-granting jewel. Obtained just this once, difficult
to acquire and easily lost, (it passes in a flash) like lightning in the
sky. Considering how (easily this can happen at any time) and realizing that all worldly activities are as (immaterial as) chaff, you must
try to extract its essence at all times, day and night. I, the yogi, have
practiced just that. You who also seek liberation, please cultivate
yourself in the same way.

11. After death, there is no guarantee that you will not be reborn in one of
the three unfortunate realms. Nevertheless, it is certain that the Three
Jewels of Refuge have the power to protect you from their terrors. For
this reason, your taking of refuge should be extremely solid and you
should follow its advice without ever letting (your commitments)
weaken. Moreover, (your success in) so doing depends on your considering thoroughly which are the black or the white karmic actions
together with their results and then living according to the guides of
what is to be adopted or rejected. I, the yogi, have practiced just that.
You who also seek liberation, please cultivate yourself in the same way.

12. The fullest strides (of progress) in actualizing the supreme paths will not
come about unless you have attained the working basis (of an ideal

human body) that is complete with (all eight ripened favorable) qualities. Therefore, you must train in the causal (virtuous actions) that will preclude (your attainment of such a form) from being incomplete. (Furthermore) as it is extremely essential to cleanse away the stains of black karmic debts and downfalls (from broken vows) tarnishing the three gateways (of your body, speech and mind), and especially (to remove) your karmic obstacles (which would prevent such a rebirth), you should cherish continually devoting yourself to (applying) the complete set of four opponent powers (which can purge you of them). I, the yogi, have practiced just that. You who also seek liberation, please cultivate yourself in the same way.

13. If you do not make an effort to think about true sufferings and their drawbacks, you will not properly develop a keen interest to work for liberation. If you do not consider the stages whereby (true) origins of all suffering place and keep you in cyclic existence, you will not know the means for cutting the root of this vicious circle. Therefore, you should cherish exuding total disgust and renunciation of such existence by knowing which factors bind you to its wheel. I, the yogi, have practiced just that. You who also seek liberation, please cultivate yourself in the same way.

14. Ever-enhancing your enlightened motive of bodhicitta is the central axle of the Mahayana path. It is the basis and foundation for great waves of (enlightening) conduct. Like a gold-making elixir, (it turns) everything (you do) into the two collections, (building up) a treasure of merit gathered from infinitely collected virtues. Knowing this, bodhisattvas hold this supreme precious mind as their innermost practice. I, the yogi, have practiced just that. You who also seek liberation, please cultivate yourself in the same way.

15. Generosity is the wish-granting jewel with which you can fulfill the hopes of sentient beings. It is the best weapon for cutting the knot of miserliness. It is the (altruistic) conduct that enhances your self-confidence and undaunted courage. It is the basis for your good reputation to be proclaimed in the ten directions. Knowing this, the wise have devoted themselves to the excellent path of completely giving away their body, belongings and merit. I, the yogi, have practiced just that. You who also seek liberation, please cultivate yourself in the same way.

16. Ethical discipline is the water that washes away the stains of faulty actions. It is the ray of moonlight that cools the scorching heat of the defilements. (It makes you) radiant like a Mount Meru in the midst of the nine kinds of being. By its power, you are able to bend all beings (to your good influence) without (recourse to) mesmerizing glares. Knowing this, the holy ones have safeguarded, as they would their eyes, the precepts that they have accepted (to keep) purely. I, the yogi, have practiced just that. You who also seek liberation, please cultivate yourself in the same way.

17. Patience is the best adornment for those with power and the perfect ascetic practice for those tormented by delusions. It is the high-soaring eagle as the enemy of the snake of anger, and the thickest armor against the weapons of abusive language. Knowing this, (the wise) have accustomed themselves in various ways and forms to the armor of supreme patience. I, the yogi, have practiced just that. You who also seek liberation, please cultivate yourself in the same way.

18. Once you wear the armor of resolute and irreversible joyous effort, your expertise in the scriptures and insights will increase like the waxing moon. You will make all your actions meaningful (for attaining enlightenment) and will bring whatever you undertake to

its intended conclusion. Knowing this, the bodhisattvas have exerted great waves of joyous effort, washing away all laziness. I, the yogi, have practiced just that. You who also seek liberation, please cultivate yourself in the same way.

19. Meditative concentration is the king wielding power over the mind. If you fix it (on one point), it remains there, immovable like a mighty Mount Meru. If you apply it, it can engage fully with any virtuous object. It leads to the great exhilarating bliss of your body and mind being made serviceable. Knowing this, yogis who are proficient have devoted themselves continuously to single-pointed concentration, which overcomes the enemy of mental wandering. I, the yogi, have practiced just that. You who also seek liberation, please cultivate yourself in the same way.

20. Profound wisdom is the eye with which to behold profound emptiness and the path by which to uproot (fundamental ignorance), the source of cyclic existence. It is the treasure of genius praised in all the scriptural pronouncements and is renowned as the supreme lamp that eliminates the darkness of closed-mindedness. Knowing this, the wise who have wished for liberation have advanced themselves along this path with every effort. I, the yogi, have practiced just that. You who also seek liberation, please cultivate yourself in the same way.

21. In (a state of) merely single-pointed meditative concentration, you do not have the insight (that gives you) the ability to cut the root of cyclic existence. Moreover, devoid of a path of calm abiding, wisdom (by itself) cannot turn back the delusions, no matter how much you analyze them. Therefore, on the horse of unwavering calm abiding, (masters) have mounted the discriminating wisdom that is totally decisive

about how things exist [or, the wisdom penetrating the depths of the ultimate mode of being]. Then, with the sharp weapon of Middle Path reasoning, devoid of extremes, they have used wide-ranging discriminating wisdom to analyze properly and destroy all underlying supports for their (cognitions) aimed at grasping for extremes. In this way, they have expanded their intelligence that has realized emptiness. I, the yogi, have practiced just that. You who also seek liberation, please cultivate yourself in the same way.

22. Once you have achieved single-pointed concentration through accustoming yourself to single-pointedness of mind, your examination then of individual phenomena with the proper analysis should itself enhance your single-minded concentration settled extremely firmly, without any wavering, on the actual way in which all things exist. Seeing this, the zealous have marveled at the attainment of the union of calm abiding and penetrative insight. Is there need to mention that you should pray (to attain it as well)? I, the yogi, have practiced just that. You who also seek liberation, please cultivate yourself in the same way.

23. (Having achieved such a union) you should meditate both on space-like emptiness while completely absorbed (in your meditation sessions) and on illusion-like emptiness when you subsequently arise. By doing this, you will, through your union of method and awareness, become praised as someone perfecting the bodhisattva's conduct. Realizing this, those with the great good fortune (to have attained enlightenment) have made it their custom never to be content with merely partial paths. I, the yogi, have practiced just that. You who also seek liberation, please cultivate yourself in the same way.

24. (Renunciation, an enlightened motive and correct view of emptiness) are necessary in common for (achieving) supreme paths through

either of the two Mahayana vehicles of (practicing) causes (for enlightenment) or (simulating now) the results (you will achieve). Therefore, once you have properly developed like this these (three principal) paths, you should rely on the skillful captain (of a fully qualified tantric master) as your protector, and set out (on this latter, speedier vehicle) across the vast ocean of the (four) classes of tantra. Those who have (done so and) devoted themselves to his or her guide-line instructions have made their attainment of (a human body with all) liberties and endowments fully meaningful (by attaining enlightenment in their very lives). I, the yogi, have practiced just that. You who also seek liberation, please cultivate yourself in the same way.

25. In order to accustom this to my own mind and also to benefit others as well who have the good fortune (to meet a true guru and be able to practice what he or she teaches), I have explained here in easily understandable words the complete path that pleases the buddhas. I pray that the merit from this may cause all sentient beings never to be parted from these pure and excellent paths. I, the yogi, have practiced just that. You who also seek liberation, please cultivate yourself in the same way.

Colophon

This concludes the *Abbreviated Points of the Graded Path to Enlightenment*, compiled in brief so that they might not be forgotten. It has been written at Ganden Nampar Gyelwa'i Monastery on Drog Riwoche Mountain, Tibet, by the Buddhist monk Losang Dragpa, a meditator who has heard many teachings.

NOTES

1. See *Atisha's Lamp for the Path to Enlightenment* for a detailed commentary by Geshe Sonam Rinchen and www.LamaYeshe.com for a brief commentary by Khunu Lama Rinpoche.

2. See *The Great Treatise on the Stages of the Path to Enlightenment* for an English translation of this text.

3. See *Opening the Eye of New Awareness*, Chapter Two.

4. See *Meditation on Emptiness*, p. 321 ff.

5. See *Meditation on Emptiness*, "Non-associated compositional factors," p. 268 ff.

6. In the present-day state of Bihar. For more information, see *The Eight Places of Buddhist Pilgrimage* on www.LamaYeshe.com.

7. See *Buddhist Advice for Living and Liberation*, verses 176 ff.

8. See *World of Tibetan Buddhism*, pp. 15–30, for a detailed discussion of the three turnings.

9. Manjushri, Vajrapani, Avalokiteshvara, Ksitigarbha, Sarvanivarana-viskambini, Akashagarbha, Maitreya and Samantabhadra.

10. The three realms are the desire, form and formless realms. The desire realm is inhabited by hell beings, hungry ghosts, animals, humans, non-gods and the first six classes of god; the form realm by the next seventeen classes of god; and the formless realm by the top four classes of god. See *Meditative States in Tibetan Buddhism* for more details.

11. See *Buddhist Advice for Living and Liberation*, verses 380–89. Also, *Essence of the Heart Sutra*, p. 42–48, for much more on Nagarjuna's

defense of the Mahayana and its origins.

12. See *Liberation in the Palm of Your Hand*, pp. 44–74, and the biography of Atisha on www.LamaYeshe.com for details of his life.

13. See *Liberation in the Palm of Your Hand*, pp. 760–61, for the lineage of these teachings.

14. See *Liberation in Our Hands, Part 1*, p. 242 ff., for details of these three lineages.

15. Generosity, ethics, forbearance, enthusiastic perseverance, concentration and wisdom.

16. Beings from any of the three realms—desire, form and formless—can be reborn into any of the three. For example, desire realm beings can be reborn into the desire, form or formless realm and so forth. Thus, there are nine kinds of being.

17. See *Liberation in Our Hands, Part 1*, p. 71, for more on this.

18. The four foundations of mindfulness, the four correct trainings, the four supports for miraculous ability, the five faculties, the five powers, the seven branches of enlightenment and the eightfold path. See *Essence of the Heart Sutra*, pp. 26–29 for an enumeration and brief explanation of these thirty-seven aspects of the path.

19. See *The Great Treatise*, Volume 1, p. 71.

20. See *World of Tibetan Buddhism*, p. 160, n. 15, for questions about the source of this frequently-quoted verse of the Buddha.

21. See *Essence of the Heart Sutra*, pp. 104–106, for a discussion of definitive versus provisional interpretation.

22. This alludes to the four reliances of not relying merely on the person, but on the words; not merely on the words but on their meaning; not merely on the provisional meaning but on the definitive meaning; and not merely on intellectual understanding of the definitive meaning but on direct, non-conceptual experience of it.

23. The eight liberties, or freedoms, are freedom from the four non-human states of rebirth in the hell, hungry ghost, animal or long-lived god realms and the four human states of rebirth when or where

the Dharma teachings do not exist or with imperfect faculties or wrong views. In none of these states do we have the freedom to practice Dharma to the full. See *Liberation in Our Hands, Part 2*, p. 73 ff. for more details.

24. Wrong livelihoods include killing or abusing sentient beings for a living, living off the proceeds of selling holy objects such as texts, statues and thangkas and so forth.

25. See, for example, His Holiness the Dalai Lama's *The Meaning of Life* for a detailed explanation of the twelve links.

26. See *World of Tibetan Buddhism*, p. 42: "Due to the existence of this, that arises; due to the production of this, that is engendered. It is thus: due to ignorance, there is the volitional action; due to action, there is consciousness," which is attributed to the *Rice Seedling Sutra (Shalistambhasutra)*.

27. Quoted in *Liberation in our Hands, Part 2*, pp. 140–141.

28. See *Abhidharmakoshabhasyam*, Chapter 3.

29. For an extremely detailed discussion of all aspects of karma, see *Liberation in Our Hands, Part 2*, Day Thirteen, p. 227 ff.

30. See *Making Life Meaningful*, p. 83 ff. for the practice of the "Bodhisattva's Confession of Moral Downfalls."

31. See *Teachings from the Vajrasattva Retreat*, p. 663.

32. See *Liberation in our Hands, Part 1*, pp. 209–213; *The Tantric Path of Purification*; and *Everlasting Rain of Nectar*.

33. See *Daily Purification: A Short Vajrasattva Practice* for a brief, easy method of purifying negativities.

34. See *Meditative States in Tibetan Buddhism* for details of the four concentrations and the four formless absorptions.

35. See *Liberation in our Hands, Part 1*, page 143, note 67.

36. See *Liberation in our Hands, Part 1*, page 143, notes 67 through 70.

37. The term unenlightened existence is used by established Theravada scholars and other academics to denote life in samsara, considering shravakas and pratyekabuddhas to have attained enlightenment,

although not the complete, fully-perfected enlightenment of buddhahood. See *Essence of the Heart Sutra*, p. 80. In *Illuminating the
Path*, we consider all sentient beings to be unenlightened; see the
relevant glossary entries.

38. See His Holiness's commentary on this in *Healing Anger*.

39. See *Liberation in Our Hands*, Part 3, pp. 256–260.

40. See *The Yogic Deeds of Bodhisattvas*, page 274, verse 348.

41. For more on the dispute between Buddhapalita and Bhavaviveka, see
Essence of the Heart Sutra, pp. 108–111.

42. For more on the four schools, see *Essence of the Heart Sutra*, pp.
99–112.

43. See *Nagarjuna's Seventy Stanzas* for a translation of this text.

44. See *Meditation on Emptiness*, p. 131 ff.

45. See His Holiness the Dalai Lama's new commentary on this text,
Essence of the Heart Sutra. See also pp. 91–97 of that work for a discussion of the four seals.

46. Heat, summit, patience and supreme Dharma.

47. See *The Three Levels of Spiritual Perfection*, p. 543, "Non-dual clarity and emptiness/voidness."

48. With thanks to Jeff Cox of Snow Lion publications for permission
to use Ruth Sonam's excellent translation in this book.

49. Translated by Sherpa Tulku, Khamlung Tulku, Alexander Berzin and
Jonathan Landaw, 1973, © LTWA, Dharamsala. This is essentially
the translation that was used during His Holiness's teachings, slight-
ly modified with reference to Dr. Berzin's revised translation on
www.berzinarchives.com. See *Door to Liberation* p. 173, for another translation of *Lines of Experience*.

Bibliography

Aryadeva. *The Yogic Deeds of Bodhisattvas: Gyel-tsap on Aryadeva's Four Hundred.* Commentary by Geshe Sonam Rinchen, translated by Ruth Sonam. Ithaca: Snow Lion Publications, 1994.

Atisha Dipamkara Shrijnana. *Atisha's Lamp for the Path to Enlightenment.* Commentary by Geshe Sonam Rinchen, translated and edited by Ruth Sonam. Ithaca: Snow Lion Publications, 1997.

Deshung Rinpoche. *The Three Levels of Spiritual Perfection.* Translated by Jared Rhoton. Boston: Wisdom Publications, 1995.

Gyatso, Geshe Jampa. *Everlasting Rain of Nectar: Purification Practice in Tibetan Buddhism.* Edited by Joan Nicell. Boston: Wisdom Publications, 1996.

Gyatso, Tenzin, His Holiness the Dalai Lama. *Essence of the Heart Sutra.* Translated and edited by Geshe Thupten Jinpa. Boston: Wisdom Publications, 2002.

——. *Healing Anger: The Power of Patience from a Buddhist Perspective.* Translated by Geshe Thupten Jinpa. Ithaca: Snow Lion Publications, 1997.

——. *The Meaning of Life from a Buddhist Perspective.* Translated and edited by Jeffrey Hopkins. Boston: Wisdom Publications, 1992.

——. *Opening the Eye of New Awareness.* Translated by Donald S. Lopez, Jr. Boston: Wisdom Publications, 1984.

——. *The World of Tibetan Buddhism: An Overview of Its Philosophy and Practice.* Translated and edited by Geshe Thupten Jinpa. Boston: Wisdom Publications, 1995.

Hopkins, Jeffrey. *Meditation on Emptiness.* Boston: Wisdom

Publications, 1983.

Lati Rinbochay and Denma Lochö Rinbochay. *Meditative States in Tibetan Buddhism.* Translated by Leah Zahler and Jeffrey Hopkins. Boston: Wisdom Publications, 1997.

Nagarjuna. *Buddhist Advice for Living and Liberation, Nagarjuna's Precious Garland.* Translated and edited by Jeffrey Hopkins. Ithaca: Snow Lion Publications, 1998.

—. *Nagarjuna's "Seventy Stanzas": A Buddhist Psychology of Emptiness.* Commentary by Geshe Sonam Rinchen, translated by Tenzin Dorjee and David Ross Komito. Ithaca: Snow Lion Publications, 1987.

Pabongka Rinpoche. *Liberation in Our Hands, Parts 1, 2 and 3.* Transcribed and edited by Yongzin Trijang Rinpoche Losang Yeshe Tenzin Gyatso, translated by Geshe Lobsang Tharchin with Artemus B. Engle. Howell: Mahayana Sutra and Tantra Press, 1990, 1994, 2001.

—. *Liberation in the Palm of Your Hand.* Translated by Michael Richards. Boston: Wisdom Publications, 1991.

Russell, Jeremy. *The Eight Places of Buddhist Pilgrimage.* New Delhi: Mahayana Publications, 1981. Out of print; available on www.LamaYeshe.com.

Shantideva. *A Guide to the Bodhisattva's Way of Life.* Translated by Stephen Batchelor. Dharamsala: Library of Tibetan Works and Archives, 1979.

—. *A Guide to the Bodhisattva's Way of Life.* Translated by Vesna A. Wallace and Alan B. Wallace. Ithaca: Snow Lion Publications, 1997.

Sopa, Geshe Lhundup and Jeffrey Hopkins. *Cutting Through Appearances: Practice and Theory of Tibetan Buddhism.* Ithaca: Snow Lion Publications, 1989.

Tsong Khapa, Lama Je. *The Great Treatise on the Stages of the Path to Enlightenment, Volume One.* Lamrim Chenmo Translation

Committee. Ithaca: Snow Lion Publications, 2000.

Vasubandhu. *Abhidharmakoshabhasyam.* Four volumes. Translated into French by Louis de La Vallée Poussin, into English by Leo M. Pruden. Berkeley: Asian Humanities Press, 1991.

Yeshe, Lama Thubten. *The Tantric Path of Purification.* Edited by Nicholas Ribush. Boston: Wisdom Publications, 1994.

Zopa Rinpoche, Lama Thubten. *Daily Purification: A Short Vajrasattva Practice.* Edited by Nicholas Ribush. Boston: Lama Yeshe Wisdom Archive, 2001.

—. *Making Life Meaningful.* Edited by Nicholas Ribush. Boston: Lama Yeshe Wisdom Archive, 2001.

—. *Teachings from the Vajrasattva Retreat.* Edited by Ailsa Cameron and Nicholas Ribush. Boston: Lama Yeshe Wisdom Archive, 2000.

FURTHER RECOMMENDED READING

Gyatso, Tenzin, His Holiness the Dalai Lama. *Path to Bliss: A Practical Guide to Stages of Meditation.* Translated by Geshe Thupten Jinpa, edited by Christine Cox. Ithaca: Snow Lion Publications, 1991. Lam-rim teachings; a commentary on Panchen Losang Chökyi Gyältsän's *Path to Bliss Leading to Omniscience.*

—. *The Path to Enlightenment.* Translated and edited by Glenn H. Mullin. Ithaca: Snow Lion Publications, 1995. Lam-rim teachings; a commentary on Sonam Gyatso, the Third Dalai Lama's *Essence of Refined Gold.*

Rabten, Geshe. *The Essential Nectar.* Translated and edited by Martin Willson. Boston: Wisdom Publications, 1992. Lam-rim teachings and meditations; translation of and contemporary commentary on a text by the eighteenth century Tibetan scholar, Yeshe Tsöndru.

Wangchen, Geshe Namgyäl. *Awakening the Mind (of Enlightenment).* Wisdom Publications, 1988. Meditations on the path to enlightenment.

Wangyel, Geshe. *The Door of Liberation.* Boston: Wisdom Publications, 1995. Teachings in the Kadam tradition.

GLOSSARY

(Skt = Sanskrit; Tib = Tibetan)

A

affliction. See *delusion.*

aggregates. See *skandha.*

arhat (Skt; Tib: dra-chom-pa). Literally, foe destroyer. A person who has destroyed his or her inner enemy, the delusions, and attained liberation from cyclic existence.

arya (Skt; Tib: phag-pa). Literally, noble. One who has realized the wisdom of emptiness.

Aryadeva. Third century Indian Buddhist philosopher and leading early proponent of Nagarjuna's Prasangika-Madhyamaka philosophy.

Asanga, Arya. Fourth century Indian Buddhist philosopher who founded the Cittamatra School of Buddhist philosophy. See *Meditation on Emptiness* p. 359.

Atisha Dipamkara Shrijnana (982–1054). The great Indian master who first formulated the lam-rim teachings when he came to Tibet in 1042. See Chapter 2 for more information.

B

bhagavan (Skt; Tib: chom-dän-dä). Epithet for a buddha; sometimes translated as Lord, Blessed One and so forth. One who has destroyed *(chom)* all defilements, possesses all qualities *(dän)* and has transcended the world *(dä).*

bhumi (Skt). Ground, or level, as in the ten bodhisattva levels. See *Meditation on Emptiness,* pp. 98–109.

bodhicitta (Skt). The altruistic intention, or determination, to reach enlightenment for the sole purpose of enlightening all sentient beings.

bodhisattva (Skt). One who possesses the compassionate motivation of bodhicitta; whose spiritual practice is directed towards the achievement of enlightenment for the sake of all sentient beings. See also *bhumi.*

Bodhisattvayana, Bodhisattva Vehicle. See *Paramitayana.*

Buddha (Skt). A fully enlightened being. One who has removed all obscurations veiling the mind and has developed all good qualities to perfection. The first of the Three Jewels of Refuge. See also *enlightenment.*

Buddhadharma (Skt). The teachings of the Buddha. See also *Dharma.*

buddhahood. See enlightenment.

buddha nature. The clear light nature of mind possessed by all sentient beings; the potential for all sentient beings to become enlightened by removing the two obscurations to liberation and omniscience. See also *obscurations,* and *Essence of the Heart Sutra,* p. 82, for more discussion on this.

Buddhist (Tib: nang-pa). One who has taken refuge in the Three Jewels of Refuge: Buddha, Dharma and Sangha and who accepts the philosophical world view of the "four seals": that all composite phenomena are impermanent, all contaminated phenomena are in the nature of suffering, all things and events are devoid of self-existence and nirvana is true peace.

C

calm abiding. See *shamatha.*

Chandrakirti. Sixth century Indian Buddhist philosopher who wrote

commentaries on Nagarjuna's philosophy. His best-known work is
A Guide to the Middle Way (Madhyamakavatara).

Cittamatra (Skt). The Mind Only School of the four schools of Buddhist
philosophy; with Madhyamaka, one of the two Mahayana schools.
See *Cutting Through Appearances* for details.

compassion (Skt: karuna). The wish for all sentient beings to be separated from their mental and physical suffering. A prerequisite for the
development of bodhicitta. Compassion is symbolized by the meditational deity Avalokiteshvara and the mantra OM MANI PADME
HUM.

consciousness. See *mind.*

constituents, eighteen (Skt: dhatu; Tib: kham). The six sense powers, the
six consciousnesses and the six objects.

cyclic existence. See *samsara.*

D

defilement. See *delusion.*

delusion (Skt: klesha; Tib: nyön-mong). Literally, "that which afflicts from
within." A delusion has the function of disturbing the mind the
moment it arises. Delusions are obscurations covering the essentially pure nature of mind, being thereby responsible for suffering and
dissatisfaction. The main delusion is ignorance, out of which grow
desirous attachment, hatred, jealousy and all the others.

dependent origination. Also called dependent arising. In general, phenomena arise in dependence upon causes and conditions and are
therefore empty of inherent existence; they are not self-existent
because they are dependent arisings. See also *twelve links.*

Dharma (Skt; Tib: chö). Spiritual teachings, particularly those of
Shakyamuni Buddha. Literally, that which protects us from suffering. The Tibetan term has the literal connotation of "changing," or

"bringing about transformation." The second of the Three Jewels of
Refuge.

dharmakaya (Skt). The "buddha-body of reality." The omniscient mind
of a fully enlightened being, which, free of all obscurations and subtle hindrances, remains meditatively absorbed in the direct perception of emptiness while simultaneously cognizing all phenomena.
The result of the complete and perfect accumulation of wisdom.
One of the four holy bodies of a buddha (see also *rupakaya* and
svabhavikakaya).

dualistic view. The ignorant view characteristic of the unenlightened
mind in which all things are falsely conceived to have concrete self-
existence. To such a view, the appearance of an object is mixed with
the false image of its being independent or self-existent, thereby
leading to further dualistic views concerning subject and object, self
and other, this and that and so forth.

E

emptiness (Skt: shunyata). The absence of the apparent independent, self-
existence of phenomena; lack of inherent existence. Sometimes
translated as "voidness." (See also *inherent existence.*)

enlightenment (Skt: bodhi; Tib: jang-chub). Full awakening; buddhahood. The
ultimate goal of Buddhist practice, attained when all limitations have
been removed from the mind and one's positive potential has been
completely and perfectly realized. It is a state characterized by infinite
compassion, wisdom and skill. See p. 14 for some discussion of this.

F

five paths. The paths along which beings progress to liberation and enlightenment; the paths of accumulation, preparation (conjunction), seeing

(insight), meditation and no more learning (beyond training). See *Liberation in Our Hands*, Part 1, p. 106, note 86.

form body. See *rupakaya.*

Four Noble Truths. The subject of the Buddha's first turning of the wheel of Dharma. The truths of suffering, the origin of suffering, the cessation of suffering and the path to the cessation of suffering as seen by an *arya.*

G

Geluk (Tib). The Virtuous Order. The order of Tibetan Buddhism founded by Lama Tsong Khapa and his disciples in the early fifteenth century and the most recent of the four main schools of Tibetan Buddhism. Developed from the Kadam School founded by Atisha and Dromtönpa. Cf. *Nyingma, Kagyü* and *Sakya.*

Great Vehicle. See *Mahayana.*

H

Hearer Vehicle. See *Shravakayana.*

Hinayana (Skt). Literally, Small, or Lesser, Vehicle. It is one of the two general divisions of Buddhism. Hinayana practitioners' motivation for following the Dharma path is principally their intense wish for personal liberation from samsara. Two types of Hinayana practitioner are identified: hearers and solitary realizers. Cf. *Mahayana.*

I

ignorance (Skt: avidya; Tib: ma-rig-pa). Literally, "not seeing" that which exists, or the way in which things exist. There are basically two kinds, ignorance of karma and ignorance of ultimate truth. The fundamental delusion from which all others spring. The first of the twelve links of dependent origination.

impermanence (Tib: mi-tag-pa). The gross and subtle levels of the transience of phenomena. The moment things and events come into existence, their disintegration has already begun.

inherent (or intrinsic) existence. What phenomena are empty of; the object of negation, or refutation. To ignorance, phenomena appear to exist independently, in and of themselves; to exist inherently. Cf. *emptiness*.

intelligence, the faculty of (Tib: nam chöd). Sometimes translated as "faculty of imagination." His Holiness uses this term in the Western sense of a human being's capacity for thinking and imagination that enables him or her to project into the future, recollect past experiences and so forth, a faculty that often leads us into conflict. The insight, or wisdom, that enables us to judge between long- and short-term benefit and detriment.

K

Kadam (Tib). The order of Tibetan Buddhism founded in the eleventh century by Atisha, Dromtönpa and their followers, the "Kadampa geshes"; the forerunner of the Geluk School.

Kagyü (Tib). The order of Tibetan Buddhism founded in the eleventh century by Marpa, Milarepa, Gampopa and their followers. One of the four main schools of Tibetan Buddhism. Cf. *Nyingma, Sakya* and *Geluk*.

Kangyur (Tib). The part of the Tibetan Canon that contains the sutras and tantras; literally, "translation of the (Buddha's) word." It contains 108 volumes.

karma (Skt; Tib: lä). Intentional (but not necessarily conscious) action; the working of cause and effect, whereby positive (virtuous) actions produce happiness and negative (non-virtuous) actions produce suffering.

kaya (Skt). Buddha-, or holy, body. A body of an enlightened being. See also *dharmakaya* and *rupakaya*.

klesha (Skt). See *delusion*.

L

lama (Tib; Skt: guru). A spiritual guide or teacher. One who shows a disciple the path to liberation and enlightenment. Literally, heavy—heavy with knowledge of Dharma.

lam-rim (Tib). The graduated path. A presentation of Shakyamuni Buddha's teachings in a form suitable for the step-by-step training of a disciple. See also *Atisha* and *three principal paths*.

Lesser Vehicle. See *Hinayana*.

liberation (Skt: nirvana, or moksha; Tib: nyang-dä, or thar-pa). The state of complete freedom from samsara; the goal of a practitioner seeking his or her own escape from suffering (see also *Hinayana*). "Lower nirvana" is used to refer to this state of self-liberation, while "higher nirvana" refers to the supreme attainment of the full enlightenment of buddhahood. Natural nirvana *(Tib: rang-zhin nyang-dä)* is the fundamentally pure nature of reality, where all things and events are devoid of any inherent, intrinsic or independent reality.

M

Madhyamaka (Skt). The Middle Way School of Buddhist philosophy; a system of analysis founded by Nagarjuna based on the *Prajnaparamita* sutras of Shakyamuni Buddha and considered to be the supreme presentation of the wisdom of emptiness. This view holds that all phenomena are dependent originations and thereby avoids the mistaken extremes of self-existence and non-existence, or eternalism and nihilism. It has two divisions, *Svatantrika* and *Prasangika*. With *Cittamatra*, one of the two Mahayana schools of philosophy. See *Cutting Through Appearances* for details.

Madhyamika (Skt). Follower of *Madhyamaka*.

Mahayana (Skt). Literally, Great Vehicle. It is one of the two general divisions of Buddhism. Mahayana practitioners' motivation for following the Dharma path is principally their intense wish for all mother sentient beings to be liberated from conditioned existence, or samsara, and to attain the full enlightenment of buddhahood. The Mahayana has two divisions, *Paramitayana* (Sutrayana) and *Vajrayana* (Tantrayana, Mantrayana). Cf. *Hinayana*.

Maitreya (Tib: Jam-pa). After Shakyamuni Buddha, the next (fifth) of the thousand buddhas of this fortunate eon to descend to turn the wheel of Dharma. Presently residing in the pure land of Tushita (Ganden). Recipient of the method lineage of Shakyamuni Buddha's teachings, which, in a mystical transmission, he passed on to Asanga.

Manjushri (Tib: Jam-päl-yang). The bodhisattva (or buddha) of wisdom. Recipient of the wisdom lineage of Shakyamuni Buddha's teachings, which he passed on to Nagarjuna.

mantra (Skt). Literally, mind protection. Mantras are Sanskrit syllables—usually recited in conjunction with the practice of a particular meditational deity—and embody the qualities of the deity with which they are associated.

mara (Skt). See *obstructive forces*.

meditation (Tib: gom). Familiarization of the mind with a virtuous object. There are two types, placement (absorptive) and analytic (insight).

merit. Positive imprints left on the mind by virtuous, or Dharma, actions. The principal cause of happiness. Accumulation of merit, when coupled with the accumulation of wisdom, eventually results in rupakaya.

Middle Way School. See *Madhyamaka.*

Milarepa (1040–1123 or 1052–1135). One of Tibet's greatest yogis, he achieved enlightenment in his lifetime under the tutelage of his guru, Marpa, who was a contemporary of Atisha. One of the founding fathers of the Kagyü School.

mind (Skt: citta; Tib: sem). Synonymous with consciousness *(Skt: vijnana; Tib: nam-she)* and sentience *(Skt: manas; Tib: yi).* Defined as that which is "clear and knowing"; a formless entity that has the ability to perceive objects. Mind is divided into six primary consciousnesses and fifty-one mental factors.

Mind Only School. See *Cittamatra.*

N

Nagarjuna. Second century Indian Buddhist philosopher who founded the Madhyamaka School of Buddhist philosophy. See *Meditation on Emptiness*, pp. 356–359.

Ngari. Western Tibet, where Atisha first arrived. He wrote his *Lamp for the Path* at the monastery of Thöling in Zhang-Zhung, or Gugé.

nihilism. The doctrine that nothing exists; that, for example, there's no cause and effect of actions or no past and future lives.

nirmanakaya (Skt). See *rupakaya.*

nirvana (Skt; Tib: nyang-dä). Literally, "beyond sorrow," that is, beyond reach of the delusions. See p.16 for a discussion of the term. See also *liberation* for more discussion.

Nyingma (Tib). The old translation school of Tibetan Buddhism, which traces its teachings back to the time of Padmasambhava, the eighth century Indian tantric master invited to Tibet by King Trisong

Detsen to clear away hindrances to the establishment of Buddhism in Tibet. The first of the four main schools of Tibetan Buddhism. Cf. *Kagyü, Sakya* and *Geluk.*

O

object of negation, or refutation (Tib: gag-cha). What is conceived by an awareness conceiving true existence; the appearance of inherent existence.

obscurations, obstructions (Skt: avarana). Gross hindrances *(Skt: klesh-avarana; Tib: nyön-drib; see also delusion),* which prevent liberation from samsara, and subtle hindrances, which prevent omniscience *(Skt: jneyavarana; Tib: she-drib).*

obstructive forces (Skt: mara), four. The afflictions, death, the five aggregates and the "divine youth demon." See pp. 95–96.

P

paramita (Skt). See *six perfections.*

Paramitayana (Skt). The Perfection Vehicle; the first of the two Mahayana paths. This is the gradual path to enlightenment traversed by bodhisattvas practicing the six perfections through the ten bodhisattva levels *(bhumi)* over countless eons of rebirth in samsara for the benefit of all sentient beings. Also called Sutrayana or Bodhisattvayana. Cf. *Vajrayana.*

path(s) of accumulation, preparation, seeing. See *five paths.*

penetrative insight. See *vipashyana.*

Perfection Vehicle. See *Paramitayana.*

Prajnaparamita (Skt). The perfection of wisdom.

Prasangika (Skt). The Middle Way Autonomy School of the four schools of Buddhist philosophy. See *Cutting Through Appearances* for details.

See also *Madhyamaka*.

pratimoksha (Skt). Vows of individual liberation; seven types. See the discussion of Verses 20 and 21 of *Lamp for the Path,* pp. 122–123.

Pratyekabuddhayana (Skt). The Solitary Realizer Vehicle. One of the branches of the Hinayana. Practitioners who strive for nirvana in solitude, without relying on a teacher. Cf. *Sharavakayana*.

preta (Skt). Hungry ghost, or spirit. The preta realm is one of the three lower realms of cyclic existence. See *Liberation in Our Hands, Part 2*, p. 161 ff. for a detailed discussion.

purification. The eradication from the mind of negative imprints left by past non-virtuous actions, which would otherwise ripen into suffering. The most effective methods of purification employ the four opponent powers of regret, reliance, virtuous activity and resolve. See p. 89.

puja (Skt). Literally, offering; usually used to describe an offering ceremony such as the *Offering to the Spiritual Master (Guru Puja)*.

R

refuge. The door to the Dharma path. Fearing the sufferings of samsara, for themselves or others, Buddhists take refuge in the Three Jewels with the faith that Buddha, Dharma and Sangha have the power to lead them to happiness, better rebirths, liberation or enlightenment.

renunciation (Tib: nge-jung). A heartfelt feeling of complete disgust with cyclic existence such that day and night one yearns for liberation and engages in the practices that secure it. The first of the three principal aspects of the path to enlightenment. Cf. *bodhicitta* and *right view*.

right view. See *emptiness*.

rinpoche (Tib). Literally, "precious one." Epithet for an incarnate lama, that is one who has intentionally taken rebirth in a human form to benefit sentient beings on the path to enlightenment.

rupakaya (Skt). The "buddha-body of form" of a fully enlightened being; the result of the complete and perfect accumulation of merit. It has two aspects—*sambhogakaya*, or "buddha-body of perfect resource," in which the enlightened mind appears to benefit highly realized bodhisattvas, and *nirmanakaya*, or "buddha-body of perfect emanation," in which the enlightened mind appears to benefit ordinary beings. See also *dharmakaya*.

S

Sakya (Tib). One of the four main schools of Tibetan Buddhism. It was founded in the eleventh century in the south of the province of Tsang by Konchog Gyälpo. Cf. *Nyingma, Kagyü* and *Geluk*.

sambhogakaya (Skt). See *rupakaya*.

Samkhya (Skt). Early non-Buddhist philosophical school; the so-called "enumerators," because they advocate a definite enumeration of the causes that produce existents. See pp.17–18.

samsara (Skt; Tib: khor-wa). The six realms of conditioned existence, three lower—hell, hungry ghost *(Skt: preta)* and animal—and three upper—human, non-god *(Skt: asura)* and god *(Skt: sura)*; the beginningless, recurring cycle of death and rebirth under the control of delusion and karma and fraught with suffering. It also refers to the contaminated aggregates of a sentient being.

Sangha (Skt). Spiritual community; the third of the Three Jewels of Refuge. Absolute Sangha are those who have directly realized emptiness; relative Sangha are ordained monks and nuns.

Sautrantika (Skt). The Sutra (Hinayana) School of the four schools of Buddhist philosophy. See *Cutting Through Appearances* for details.

sentient being (Tib: sem-chen). Any unenlightened being; any being whose mind is not completely free from gross and subtle ignorance.

Shakyamuni Buddha (563–483 BC). Fourth of the one thousand founding buddhas of this present world age. Born a prince of the Shakya
clan in north India, he taught the sutra and tantra paths to liberation and enlightenment; founder of what came to be known as
Buddhism. (From the *Skt: buddha*—"fully awake.")

shamatha (Skt; Tib: shi-nä). Calm abiding; stabilization arisen from
meditation and conjoined with special pliancy. See, for example,
Meditation on Emptiness, pp. 67–90.

Shantideva. Eighth century Indian Buddhist philosopher and bodhisattva who propounded the Madhyamaka Prasangika view wrote the
quintessential Mahayana text, *A Guide to the Bodhisattva's Way of
Live (Bodhicharyavatara)*.

Shravakayana (Skt). The Hearer Vehicle. One of the branches of the
Hinayana. Practitioners (hearers, or *shravakas*) who strive for nir-
vana on the basis of listening to teachings from a teacher. Cf.
Pratyekabuddhayana.

six perfections (Skt: paramita). Generosity, ethical discipline, forbearance,
enthusiastic perseverance, concentration and wisdom. See also
Paramitayana.

skandha (Skt). The five psychophysical constituents that make up a sentient being: form, feeling, discriminative awareness, conditioning
(compositional) factors and consciousness.

Solitary Realizer Vehicle. See *Pratyekabuddhayana*.

sources, twelve (Skt: ayatana; Tib: kye-che). The six internal sources (of
consciousness) are the eye, ear, nose, tongue, body and mental sense
powers; the six external sources (of consciousness or fields of consciousness) are the form source, sound source, odor source, taste
source, object-of-touch source and phenomenon source.

sutra (Skt). A discourse of Shakyamuni Buddha; the pre-tantric division
of Buddhist teachings stressing the cultivation of bodhicitta and the

practice of the six perfections. See also *Paramitayana*.

Sutrayana (Skt). See *Paramitayana*.

svabhavikakaya (Skt). The buddha-body of nature; the emptiness of the dharmakaya. See *Liberation in Our Hands, Part 2*, p. 289.

Svatantrika (Skt). The Middle Way Autonomy School of the four schools of Buddhist philosophy. It has two divisions, *Yogachara-Svatantrika* and *Sautrantika-Svatantrika*. See *Cutting Through Appearances* for details. See also *Madhyamaka*.

T

tantra (Skt; Tib: gyü). Literally, thread, or continuity; the texts of the secret mantra teachings of Buddhism. Often used to refer to these teachings themselves. See also *Vajrayana*. Cf. *sutra*.

Tantrayana (Skt). See *Vajrayana*.

Tengyur (Tib). The part of the Tibetan Canon that contains the Indian pandits' commentaries on the Buddha's teachings. Literally, "translation of the commentaries." It contains about 225 volumes (depending on the edition).

ten non-virtuous actions. Three of body (killing, stealing, sexual misconduct); four of speech (lying, speaking harshly, divisive speech and gossiping); and three of mind (covetousness, ill will and wrong views). General actions to be avoided so as not to create negative karma.

Theravada (Skt). One of the eighteen schools into which the Hinayana split not long after Shakyamuni Buddha's death; the dominant Hinayana school today, prevalent in Thailand, Sri Lanka and Burma, and well represented in the West.

three baskets. See *tripitaka*.

Three Higher Trainings. Morality (ethics), meditation (concentration) and wisdom (insight).

Three Jewels (Tib: kon-chog-sum). The objects of Buddhist refuge. Buddha, Dharma and Sangha.

three principal paths (or, three principal aspects of the path). The three main divisions of the lam-rim: renunciation, bodhicitta and the right view (of emptiness).

tripitaka (Skt). The three divisions of the Dharma into vinaya, sutra and abhidharma.

Triple Gem. See *Three Jewels.*

Tsong Khapa, Lama Je (1357–1417). Founder of the Geluk tradition of Tibetan Buddhism and revitalizer of many sutra and tantra lineages and the monastic tradition in Tibet.

twelve links of dependent origination. The twelve steps in the evolution of cyclic existence: ignorance, karmic formation, consciousness, name and form, sensory fields, contact, feelings, attachment, grasping, becoming (existence), birth and aging and death.

V

Vaibhashika (Skt). The Great Exposition (Hinayana) School of the four schools of Buddhist philosophy. See *Cutting Through Appearances* for details.

Vajrayana (Skt). The adamantine vehicle; the second of the two Mahayana paths; also called Tantrayana or Mantrayana. This is the quickest vehicle of Buddhism as it allows certain practitioners to attain enlightenment within a single lifetime. See also *tantra.*

vinaya (Skt). The Buddha's teachings on ethical discipline (morality), monastic conduct and so forth; one of the three baskets.

vipashyana (Skt). Penetrative (special) insight; a wisdom of thorough discrimination of phenomenon conjoined with special pliancy induced by the power of analysis. See, for example, *Meditation on Emptiness,* pp. 91–109.

vows of individual liberation. See *pratimoksha.*

W

wisdom. Different levels of insight into the nature of reality. There are, for example, the three wisdoms of hearing, contemplation and meditation. Ultimately, there is the wisdom realizing emptiness, which frees beings from cyclic existence and eventually brings them to enlightenment. The complete and perfect accumulation of wisdom results in dharmakaya. Cf. *merit.*

Y

Yogachara (Skt). Branch of Madhyamaka-Svatantrika School; its followers assert a coarse selflessness of phenomena that is the same as the Cittamatrins' subtle selflessness of phenomena—the lack of difference in entity between subject and object.

Thubten Dhargye Ling ("Land of Flourishing Dharma") is a center for the study and practice of Tibetan Buddhism. It was founded in 1978 by Geshe Tsultim Gyeltsen, who gives regular teachings on Buddhist texts and classes in meditation.

Over the years, Geshe Gyeltsen has invited many eminent masters to teach at his center, including Kyabje Song Rinpoche and Lati Rinpoche. Thubten Dhargye Ling has also sponsored four visits to Los Angeles by His Holiness the Dalai Lama.

In 1984, His Holiness taught Lama Tsong Khapa's *The Three Principal Aspects of the Path* and gave an Avalokiteshvara initiation. In 1989 His Holiness taught Togme Zangpo's *Thirty-seven Practices of a Bodhisattva* and conferred the Kalachakra initiation. In 1997, he gave a commentary on Nagarjuna's *Precious Garland* and a Shakyamuni Buddha initiation. This book contains the teachings His Holiness gave on his fourth visit, in June, 2000, on Atisha's *Lamp for the Path to Enlightenment* and Lama Tsong Khapa's *Lines of Experience*.

Thubten Dhargye Ling
3500 East 4th Street
Long Beach, CA 90804, USA
(562) 621 9865
www.tdling.com

LAMA YESHE WISDOM ARCHIVE

The Lama Yeshe Wisdom Archive is honored and delighted to be working with Thubten Dhargye Ling Publications on this exceptionally auspicious project, His Holiness the Dalai Lama's teachings given in Los Angeles in June, 2000, *Illuminating the Path*.

The Archive was established by Lama Thubten Zopa Rinpoche in 1996 to manage the collected works of Lama Thubten Yeshe and Lama Zopa Rinpoche. At present it contains more than 7,000 cassette tapes of the Lamas' teachings going back to the early 1970s, when they began teaching Dharma to Westerners at Kopan Monastery, Kathmandu, Nepal.

The work of the Archive falls into two categories, archiving and dissemination. The archiving part includes collection and preservation of recorded material, including digitization of tapes, transcription of untranscribed tapes and management of transcripts. Dissemination mainly entails editing of checked transcripts for publication and distribution of edited material. We prepare manuscripts for publication as books for the trade, articles for various magazines and booklets for free distribution and for access through our Web site.

Several free booklets are currently available, as mentioned at the front of this book. You will also find many teachings on our Web site, www.lamayeshe.com. The Archive is a section of the Foundation for the Preservation of the Mahayana Tradition (FPMT).

For copies of our free booklets or more information, please contact

Lama Yeshe Wisdom Archive
PO Box 356, Weston, MA 02493, USA
Tel. (781) 899-9587
info@LamaYeshe.com
www.LamaYeshe.com

What to do with Dharma teachings

The Buddhadharma is the true source of happiness for all sentient beings. Books like the one in your hand show you how to put the teachings into practice and integrate them into your life, whereby you get the happiness you seek. Therefore, anything containing Dharma teachings or the names of your teachers is more precious than other material objects and should be treated with respect. To avoid creating the karma of not meeting the Dharma again in future lives, please do not put books (or other holy objects) on the floor or underneath other stuff, step over or sit upon them, or use them for mundane purposes. They should be kept in a clean, high place, separate from worldly writings, and wrapped in cloth when being carried around. These are but a few considerations.

Should you need to get rid of Dharma materials, they should not be thrown in the rubbish but burned in a special way. Briefly: do not incinerate such materials with other trash, but alone, and as they burn, recite the mantra OM AH HUM. As the smoke rises, visualize that it pervades all of space, carrying the essence of the Dharma to all sentient beings in the six samsaric realms, purifying their minds, alleviating their suffering, and bringing them all happiness, up to and including enlightenment. Some people might find this practice a bit unusual, but it is given according to tradition. Thank you very much.

Dedication

Through the merit created by preparing, reading, thinking about and sharing this book with others, may all teachers of the Dharma live long and healthy lives, may the Dharma spread throughout the infinite reaches of space, and may all sentient beings quickly attain enlightenment.

In whichever realm, country, area or place this book may be, may there be no war, drought, famine, disease, injury, disharmony or unhappiness, may there be only great prosperity, may everything needed be easily obtained, and may all be guided by only perfectly qualified Dharma teachers, enjoy the happiness of Dharma, have love and compassion for all sentient beings, and only benefit and never harm each other.

His Holiness Tenzin Gyatso, the Fourteenth Dalai Lama, is head of state and spiritual leader of Tibet. He was born on July 6, 1935, in the village of Taktser in Amdo, northeast Tibet, to a peasant family and recognized at the age of two, in accordance with Tibetan tradition, as the reincarnation of his predecessor, the Thirteenth Dalai Lama. He was enthroned on February 22, 1940, in Lhasa, the capital of Tibet, began his education at the age of six and received his *geshe lharam* degree in 1959.

On November 17, 1950, he was called upon to assume full political power after the Chinese army invaded Tibet. His efforts to bring about a peaceful resolution to Sino-Tibetan conflict were thwarted by Beijing's ruthless policy in Eastern Tibet, which ignited a popular uprising and resistance. On March 10, 1959, a massive popular demonstration in Lhasa was brutally crushed by the Chinese army. His Holiness escaped to India, where he was given political asylum. Some 80,000 Tibetan refugees followed him, and today, there are more than 120,000 Tibetans in exile. Since 1960, His Holiness has resided in Dharamsala, India, where the seat of the Tibetan Government-in-exile is now located.

Over the decades, His Holiness has worked tirelessly, with wisdom and compassion, to find a non-violent solution to Tibet's differences with China, visiting more than fifty countries, meeting politicians, religious leaders and educators in order to explain the truth of Tibet. In 1989, he received the Nobel Peace Prize in recognition of his efforts to find a peaceful end to China's brutal occupation of his country.

Many of His Holiness's teachings and writings have been published in books, articles and other media. A recent book, *The Art of Happiness*, spent more than a year on the *New York Times* bestseller list. See www.snowlion-pub.com for a complete list of His Holiness's books in print.

His Holiness often says, "I am a simple Buddhist monk; no more, no less," and indeed follows the life of monk. Living in a small cottage in Dharamsala, he rises at 3:30 in the morning to meditate, pursues a busy, ongoing schedule of administrative meetings, private audiences and religious teachings and ceremonies throughout the day, and retires with further prayer at 8:30 in the evening. He is a perfect example for us all.

Geshe Thupten Jinpa is a Tibetan geshe and a former member of Ganden Monastic University. He holds a B.A. and a Ph.D., both from the University of Cambridge, where he also worked as a research fellow. Since 1986 Jinpa has been the principal translator for His Holiness the Dalai Lama, and has translated and edited many books by His Holiness. His most recent work is *Self, Reality and Reason in Tibetan Philosophy: Tsongkhapa's Quest for the Middle Way* (Routledge Curzon, London & New York, 2002). He is currently the president of the Institute of Tibetan Classics, which is dedicated to translating key Tibetan classics into contemporary languages (see www.tibetanclassics.org). He lives in Montreal with his wife and two young daughters.

Rebecca McClen Novick is a writer and documentary filmmaker. She is the co-producer of "Strange Spirit," an award-winning film about human rights in Tibet and author of *Fundamentals of Tibetan Buddhism* (The Crossing Press, 1999).

Nicholas Ribush, M.B, B.S., is director of the Lama Yeshe Wisdom Archive. A former Australian physician and a student of Tibetan Buddhism since 1972, he co-founded Wisdom Publications with Lama Yeshe in 1975. Over the years, he has edited and published many teachings by His Holiness the Dalai Lama, Lama Yeshe, Lama Zopa Rinpoche and other Tibetan lamas.